AN *8* DAY IGNATIAN RETREAT

for Priests, Religious, Deacons, and Lay Ministers

THOMAS P. RAUSCH, SJ

Paulist Press
New York/Mahwah, NJ

Cover design by Sharyn Banks
Book design by Lynn Else

Library of Congress Cataloging-in-Publication Data

Rausch, Thomas P.
    An 8 day Ignatian retreat for priests, religious, deacons, and lay ministers / Thomas P. Rausch.
       p. cm.
    Includes bibliographical references and index.
    ISBN-13: 978-0-8091-4499-0 (alk. paper)
    1. Ignatius, of Loyola, Saint, 1491–1556. Exercitia spiritualia. 2. Spiritual exercises. 3. Spiritual retreats. I. Title: Eight day Ignatian retreat for priests, religious, deacons, and lay ministers. II. Title.
    BX2179.L8R38 2008
    269'.69—dc22

2007016475

Published by Paulist Press
997 Macarthur Boulevard
Mahwah, New Jersey 07430

www.paulistpress.com

Printed and bound in the
United States of America

CONTENTS

CONTENTS

Elliott A. Short

In memoriam

INTRODUCTION

One of the great treasurers of the Church is St. Ignatius of Loyola's famous little book, the *Spiritual Exercises*. It is not however a book designed to be read; it is intended to be of assistance to retreat directors, guiding retreatants through the Exercises, ideally for the full thirty days. Many priests, deacons, religious, and other ministers who make annual retreats do so with a director; others don't have the opportunity to do so. But all of them can find nourishment through the dynamics that structure the Exercises.

An 8 Day Ignatian Retreat for Priests, Religious, Deacons, and Lay Ministers is designed for them. It is intended as an introduction to some of the principal themes of the *Exercises*. It does not present them methodically, following the exact outline given us by St. Ignatius. Rather, it seeks to guide the retreatant into Ignatian prayer using some of the texts and contemplations from the *Exercises* as well as other images and stories that might lead a retreatant into the considerations and reflections at the heart of an Ignatian retreat.

The book is divided into the eight days of the retreat. The chapters are deliberately short; they represent a preparation for prayer, not to instruct but to move the imagination and hopefully the heart. Each presents mysteries from the life of Jesus and considerations that correspond to the dynamics of the Exercises. Take it day by day. You might want to stop with a particular gospel passage or theme, or bring in some of the related passages. Move slowly. There is no need to finish the chapter or exercise immediately. Ignatius advises the retreatant to stay where he or she finds fruit, without being anxious to pass on until satisfied (no. 76). The last chapter offers additional scripture texts that can be used for prayer.

In citing the text of the *Spiritual Exercises*, I have frequently paraphrased in an effort to make its sixteenth-century language more inclusive. Paragraph numbers refer to the critical edition in the volume on the *Exercises* in the *Monumenta Historica Societatis Jesu*.[1] In cases where I have cited a modern translation, I have acknowledged it.

Notes

1. *Monumenta Ignatiana*, Series Secunda, *Exercitia Spiritualia* (Rome: Institutum Historicum Socitatis Jesu, 1969); a good contemporary translation is Louis J. Puhl, *The Spiritual Exercises of St. Ignatius: Based on Studies in the Language of the Autograph* (Chicago: Loyola Press, 1951).

BEGINNING THE RETREAT

When the apostles return from their first mission, exhausted from their efforts and sought out by great a number of people seeking their care, Jesus tells them, "Come away to a deserted place all by yourselves and rest a while" (Mark 6:31). The disciples need rest, and are looking forward to some time in a quiet place where they can be alone with Jesus. But it is not to be. The people, knowing where they are going, get there first, and Jesus in his compassion tells the disciples, "Send them away so that they may go into the surrounding country and villages and buy something for themselves to eat" (Mark 6:36).

As a minister, you have often had this experience. Ministry brings with it many demands. But now, as you enter your retreat, you are indeed free to be with Jesus, and it is he who wants to feed you. As you begin your retreat, let me suggest three points based on the *Spiritual Exercises* of St. Ignatius: generosity, interior freedom, and confidence.

Generosity

In the *Annotaciones* or directions Ignatius gives to the director of the Exercises, he says, "It will be very profitable for the one who is to go through the exercise to enter upon them with magnanimity and generosity towards his Creator and Lord and to offer Him his entire will and liberty." Ignatius is inviting the retreatant to enter the Exercises in a generous spirit. Why not? You have nothing to do but open yourself generously to the gracious God who continues to draw you. It's good to start without an agenda, without special projects. It's not a time to catch up on your reading. Let the Lord show you what he will.

This time of retreat is a holy time; it is your time. And it is God's. So enter into it generously; let the Lord lead you.

Interior Freedom

At the opening of the first week that begins the retreat, Ignatius presents a consideration known as the First Principle and Foundation. It is worth considering in its entirety:

> We are created to praise, reverence, and serve God our Lord, and by this means to save our souls. All other things on the face of the earth are created for us, to help us in prosecuting the end for which we were created. From this it follows that we are to use them as much as they help us towards our end, and rid ourselves of them so far as they become a hindrance.
>
> Thus it is necessary to make ourselves indifferent to all created things in all that is allowed to the choice of our free will and is not prohibited to it; so that, on our part, we do not want health rather than sickness, riches rather than poverty, honor rather than dishonor, a long life rather than a short one, and so in all the rest, desiring and choosing only what is most conducive for us to the end for which we are created. (no. 23)

The language may sound strange to us. Wilkie Au and Noreen Cannon Au speak of its "philosophical and jejune wording," but they also note that Ignatius "would allow only those who had internalized its truth to begin the retreat in search of what *specific* life path would best allow them to 'praise, reverence, and serve God.'"[1] In urging the retreatant to indifference in regard to creatures, Ignatius does not mean that we do not have likes and dislikes, still less that we don't care for those who are close to us. What he intends is to bring us to that interior freedom without which we cannot really be open to God, to help us recognize any inordinate attachments that could influence a decision.

This principle should apply, not just to the way we approach our choices, decisions, and goals, but also to our prayer. Can we open ourselves up to the mystery of God's presence? Are we ready to receive whatever the Lord has in store for us? As one of the wise sisters on our campus says, we should not be seeking "the consolations of God, but the God of all consolation."

Indifference means being willing to go where the Lord may want to lead us. We should not have forbidden areas, nondiscussible issues, places we are afraid to visit. Sometimes those forbidden areas surface in our dreams, or are suggested by a recurring image, or lurk at the corners of our consciousness. It is usually difficult for us to enter these areas. We want to remain in control. We are afraid God might ask something of us we are not willing or able to give. So we hesitate, or deny, or ignore. If the Spirit leads you into one of those areas, don't be fearful. God is with you. Would the God who so loves us have in mind for us anything but what is for our happiness and good?

Confidence

Finally, we should begin a retreat with a great confidence in God's love. Ignatius reminds the retreat director that the real director is the Lord who works in the retreatant's heart. The director is just a guide or companion. Therefore he or she should not seek to move the retreatant toward any particular decision or way of life; rather the director "should permit the Creator to deal directly with the creature, and the creature directly with his

Creator and Lord" (no. 15). This should give the one beginning retreat great confidence, for God does not abandon those who truly seek him (cf. Luke 11:5–13). Perhaps it is only when we have that deep experience that Jesus has forgiven our sins, taken them on himself, so that we might be free, that we begin to appreciate something of God's incredible love for us.

How will you encounter the God who speaks in silence during this retreat? Perhaps you will encounter him in silent awe and adoration; maybe in that profound inner longing that comes from your deepest desires; sometimes with a deep peace and joy that witnesses to God's presence within you. Be patient and trust; keep watching, remain in quiet hope. Make your own the prayer of the young Samuel, "Speak, LORD, for your servant is listening" (1 Sam 3:9).

Notes

1. Wilkie Au and Noreen Cannon Au, *The Discerning Heart: Exploring the Christian Path* (Mahwah, NJ: Paulist Press, 2006), 147.

DAY 1

THE PLACE WHERE YOU STAND IS HOLY GROUND

Exodus 3:1–7

The story of Moses before the burning bush on Mount Horeb is a wonderful symbol of the encounter with God. The words, "remove the sandals from your feet, for the place on which you are standing is holy ground" (Exod 3:5), are particularly appealing for they put us in touch with our own desires to be in the presence of the sacred, to encounter the hidden God, to sense God's nearness. In Moses' fascination with the burning bush, we have a sense of what Rudolf Otto called the *mysterium fascinans et tremendum,* the frightening but awe inspiring presence of the sacred.[1]

Our own culture, with its egalitarian and leveling spirit, has tended to domesticate the holy. God doesn't seem very awe-inspiring to us, as much of God's mystery has been taken away. Our culture has replaced the incomprehensible God of the Bible and the mystical tradition with a God made very much in our own image. Just look at the language we use today, not "the Lord" or "the Almighty," but "the God I am comfortable with," or "my personal God," or "Yahweh," using the personal name which the Israelites were afraid even to pronounce. God becomes a companion and friend, almost a kind of pal, easily a "New Age" god, not the God of Moses or Jesus. We forget that to approach the holy is to be changed, as Jacob was changed, with his dislocated hip, after wrestling with the angel (Gen 32:24–25).

In an article entitled "The Eclipse of Love for God," Edward Vacek lamented the loss of a passion for God, the sense that the love of God was a value in itself, not because it makes us feel better.[2] Our therapeutic culture wants a therapeutic God, one who helps us to become self-actualized, who makes us fully functioning persons, a comforting and healing God, not one before whom we stand in awe.

The biblical tradition gives us a much different picture of the holy. To look on God directly, to see God's face is to die (Exod 33:20). Think of the biblical theophanies. When God appears to Moses on Sinai, thunder and lightning fill the sky, the holy mountain is covered with a dense cloud, and the people are forbidden to touch even its base (Exod 19). In 2 Samuel 6:6, as the ark of the covenant is being carried to Jerusalem, Uzzah is struck dead when he reaches out to steady it. In the mysterious story of the transfiguration, Jesus takes Peter, James, and John, his closest companions, to the top of a high mountain to pray, and is transfigured before them. The disciples are terrified by the vision and the cloud that overshadows them. They are in the presence of God, and they are afraid.

Many years ago, in Israel for a summer program, I remember being put off by many of the "holy places." Most of them struck me as over commercialized and of dubious historical value. We even visited a place said to house the stone Jesus used to mount the donkey on Palm Sunday. But a visit to Mount Tabor, traditional site of the transfiguration with its basilica, was different. Mount Tabor is spectacular, rising by itself out of the Plain of Esdraelon. We got to the top of the mountain just before twilight.

I remember wandering around in silence, looking down on the neatly cultivated green fields far below and over toward Nazareth where we had been earlier in the afternoon. I don't know if what we call the transfiguration happened on Mount Tabor. But my one thought in the quiet dusk of that evening was that this was a holy place, and I knew with a deeply felt certainty that Jesus, who had grown up only a few miles away, would have come himself to the top of this mountain to pray. Indeed, he may have stood where I was standing then. I was deeply moved, and will always remember the liturgy we celebrated in the lower level of the basilica.

The desire for the holy, for God, is what first drew us to a life of discipleship or ministry, perhaps to priesthood or religious life, and it is still present, though often deeply buried beneath the routines and distractions that make up our lives. We desire to experience the living God, the one who called us and whose mysterious presence still draws us forward toward the mystery.

Perhaps this tendency to domesticate the holy is one of the reasons that although religion is not popular today, spirituality is, even with people who aren't particularly religious. In the past, spirituality was something for the professionally religious, for monks and nuns, not for ordinary people. But if in our times spirituality has been rediscovered, it has also been both secularized and too often privatized. It's not just for religious people any more, but for anyone interested in the depth dimensions of their lives. That of course is all to the good.

But too often the way the term is used today, it does not have anything to do with religion. Spirituality is seen as private and personal; religion is dismissed as institutional, formal, ritualistic, and authoritarian. A regular program of physical exercise is described as spirituality; so are various twelve-step programs. The modern tendency is to separate spirituality from institutional religion and traditional Christian faith.

Thus, spirituality has been privatized, made not just personal, but individualistic. Experience is more important than doctrine; personal allegiances are fluid; religious authorities are suspect; and many create their own spiritualities, combining elements and practices from different traditions and cultures. I hear many speaking of "finding my own spirituality" or "a God I am comfortable with." Of course what is only private or personal we can control. Behind this often lurks the autonomous self. Princeton's Robert Wuthnow questions the idea of a spirituality pursued outside organized religion. Such spiritualities often seem irrational, based on self-indulgent fantasizing, or essentially private, personally invented sets of beliefs and practices. When books like *Chicken Soup for the Soul* and *The Celestine Prophecy* pass for spirituality, serious-minded observers of American religion are concerned "because they provide ready-made answers for the small setbacks and petty anxieties of ordinary life but do not speak of a righteous God who demands any thing of believers."[3] How different is the God of Jesus.

Another problem with this privatization of spirituality is that it forgets that the holy, the mystery of the divine, is always mediated to us communally. That is the great lesson of the Judaeo-Christian tradition, that God's self-disclosure takes place through the community of his people.

For Israel, Yahweh was present in certain sacred places: on Mount Horeb, on the holy mountain of Sinai, certainly in the great Temple of Jerusalem. In the psalms we can still sense the joy of the people in coming into the Temple, the place where God dwells: "I was glad when they said to me, 'Let us go to the house of the LORD'" (Ps 122:1) or their sense for God's mysterious presence: "How lovely is your dwelling place, O LORD of hosts!" (Ps 84:1); "One thing I asked of the LORD, that will I seek after: to live in the house of the LORD all the days of my life" (Ps 27:4).

There was no holy mountain, temple, or tabernacle space for the early Christians. They had no churches but would meet for worship in the home of one of the members of the community. The community itself was the sacred space, the place of

God's presence. God has sanctified the disciples in Christ; they have become the "body of Christ" (1 Cor 12:27). In 1 Corinthians 11:28–32, when Paul rebukes the Corinthians for not discerning the body, the text could be interpreted as referring either to the bread and wine of the Eucharist or to the community itself; Paul obviously means both. Similarly, in the first millennium, the "real body of Christ" was the Christian community, the "mystical body of Christ" the bread of the Eucharist. The community is also "God's building" (1 Cor 3:9); it is "a holy temple in the Lord" and "a dwelling place for God" (Eph 2:22). The community is "a royal priesthood, a holy nation, God's own people" (1 Pet 2:9).

It is interesting to trace the development in the language for church. In the New Testament, "church" is always the community, whether gathered in someone's house, as the local church, or used universally. The actual building—in the earliest days, someone's home—is a "house for the church." It was only after Constantine's legitimating Christianity in the early third century that Christians began building their own places of worship, taking over the form of the Roman basilica. Before long, the building where the church would come together is itself being called "the house of God" or "church."

At the same time, I'm always grateful that we have beautiful chapels and churches in our Catholic tradition. In his *New Seeds of Contemplation,* Thomas Merton wrote: "Let there always be quiet, dark churches in which [people] can take refuge. Places where they can kneel in silence. Houses of God filled with His silent presence."[4] We need such places. We are not just intellectual creatures; we have emotional depths that are touched by color, light, music, and shadow; the configuring of space by architectural form, art, and symbol. These elements can come together to sacralize space, make it holy, open us to the mystery of the transcendent. Chapels and churches should be designed with this in mind; those that create a sacred space draw us easily into prayer.

I had an experience of this not long ago when I was teaching in Germany. On a very cold and rainy afternoon we had an unbelievably fine tour of the Kölner Dom, the cathedral that dominates the city of Cologne. Begun in 1248, the nave and front of the church were not completed until 1880. With its enormously tall towers, second only to the Ulmer Munster (finished in 1890), it was for a while the tallest building in the world and still is its fifth largest church. The first hour was an exploration of the cathedral floor and its art, particularly its golden shrine supposedly housing the relics of the Three Kings which once drew thousands of pilgrims. Without the sun streaming through its multihued windows, the cathedral was not at its best advantage.

But the greatest part of the tour was still to come. We had another guide, a student of art history who took our group up an outside elevator, first to the arched steel structure of the roof constructed over the high ceiling of the church, and then up several narrow flights of stairs to the top of the smaller tower that surmounts the crossing. Huddled there on that great height, with snow now blowing across the platform, the city and great mass of the cathedral lay beneath us; the Hauptbanhof, one of the busiest train stations in Europe; the Rhine flanking the city and sweeping away to the horizon on either side. In the distance was a long low hill, constructed from the rubble of the devastated city in the postwar reconstruction.

We then began the long descent by foot, following catwalks through the buttresses, down spiral staircases built into the walls, walking along the triforium just below the upper clerestory windows. By this time it was dark outside, but the cathedral—lit by candles, the great organ playing, worshippers far below—was truly magic, an expression of medieval faith that still spoke in its architecture, its art, its height commanding the city, and the people praying in its candle-lit interior—a holy place.

So where is the holy place for us, the place where we remove our sandals and stand in reverence and awe before the living God? We all have places that for us are holy, places of quiet and presence. It is good to be able to retreat to such a place.

But in reality, wherever we pause to seek the Lord can be a holy place, a place of encounter where the sacred is symbolized: the place where we sit for prayer and reflection, our prayer corner, with candle and book, perhaps an icon; or a path with a view that lifts our spirits; or the gathering of our community in liturgical prayer, where God is present in word and symbol and sacrament. Perhaps it is the place where we minister, seeking to be God's hands and heart for others. These are holy places, where we can take off our sandals and open up our hearts.

Reflection Questions

1. What are my earliest experiences of God and God's presence?

2. Where have I experienced the holy in my life more recently?

3. Where do I find myself at as I begin this retreat?

PRAYER AND MINISTRY
Luke 3:21–22

In a fine article entitled "The Eclipse of Love for God," Edward Vacek begins by narrating the following: "When David Hare interviewed clergy as part of his research for his play, 'Racing Demons,' he ran into a problem: None of the priests wanted to talk about God."[5] How strange, men whose office or vocation is to be prayer leaders and mediators of the sacred, unwilling to talk about God. Vacek goes on to argue in his article that the love of God itself today is in jeopardy. Asking his students "what do you mean by love for God," most respond that it means helping one's neighbor, or keeping the commandments, or ministering to the poor, or caring for one's deepest self, or simply seeking the truth. But very few could give expression to the idea that God is to be loved for who he is, that one could be in a personal relationship with God, or that such a relationship is something to be cultivated.

Even more startling to me were some comments in a very interesting book I read recently by Raymond Hedin, entitled *Married to the Church*. Hedin, a former seminarian from Milwaukee, is presently a professor of American Literature at Indiana University. His book grew from a 1985 reunion of his seminary class. Frustrated with the pressure to publish more impersonal academic articles, and still feeling the pull of his seminary years with its camaraderie, its sense of purpose, its rootedness and security in a world of meaning taken for granted—despite the fact that he had long since left the Church and with it the Catholicism of his youth—he decided to write a much more personal book about those of his classmates who stayed the course, were ordained in 1969, and still remained priests.

The result is a fascinating study of a group of men struggling with all issues faced by priests today: celibacy, authority, retrenchment in the church after the heady days of Vatican II, an increasingly restive and independent laity, a consequent loss of status, low pay, and today we might add the humiliation brought on by the clergy sexual abuse scandal. But it was his remarks on the religious experience of his former classmates that most struck me. He writes that one of the most basic changes his classmates have experienced since ordination is what he calls "the loss of God." It is not that they have turned to disbelief in any fundamental way or bought into a new feminine image of God, as much of contemporary theology would have. "God has become for many of them not wholly impersonal, but somehow less personal, less involved with them as individuals, less the motivational center of their ministry."[6]

Some of their reflections suggest a maturation in their experience. Hedin describes it as a question of metaphor. God is no longer the stern judge of their youth, the omniscient God of the rules. Their God is a God beyond images. One priest described God as "a force, energy, being, a live being I don't know how to define," one who "laughs and doesn't take life all that seriously."[7]

But at the same time there is a definite loss of God as a personal Lord, one who is close. Perhaps this was most evident in the area of their prayer, for he says that few of his former classmates "claim an active and satisfying prayer life, and even when they do, they describe it more often than not as getting in touch with a higher power rather than as praying to a personal God."[8]

In an address on the priesthood, Cardinal Joseph Bernardin once remarked that a priest must be in habitual contact with the divine mystery, standing stubbornly in the presence of God. "He must take with utmost seriousness the command of St. Paul to pray continually, to orient the whole of his being to the love of God."[9]

Familiarity with God

What is true for priests is true for others in ministry as well. How can one who has no time for private prayer speak authentically of God? How can one help others to pray if he or she does not face daily the mystery of God in prayer? How can we speak of God if we are not familiar with God ourselves?

Christianity is not a message or revelation about a God who remains distant. In Augustine's words, God is more intimate to me than I am to myself, for God dwells within us. But we do not always recognize this divine indwelling. It is not God's distance, but God's very nearness that makes it so hard for us to be aware of God's presence. God surrounds us more closely than the air we breathe. Prayer puts us in touch with that divine life. It nourishes our life in God just as the gentle rain falling on the earth softens it and makes it fertile.

Prayer is familiarity with God, not the God of clichés and platitudes, but the One who creates and sustains us, the mysterious Other who is also the Abba of Jesus, the God who speaks more in silence than in words. This is the God who sometimes confronts us, the God who speaks his own inner word to us in Jesus. In a charming passage, in an instruction on prayer, Tertullian (d.c. 229) describes prayer as the universal response of creatures to their creator:

> All the angels pray. Every creature prays. Cattle and wild beasts pray and bend the knee. As they come from their barns and caves they look up to heaven and call out, lifting up their spirit in their own fashion. The birds too rise and lift themselves up to heaven: they

open out their wings, instead of hands, in the form of a cross, and give voice to what seems to be a prayer.[10]

There are many forms of prayer, but in its most basic nature all prayer is an opening of ourselves to God; it is raising our minds and hearts to God. Or, in that wonderful image of Henri Nouwen, to pray is to relax, to let go, to open one's hand and spread out one's palm in a gesture of receiving.[11] We pray in expectation because God is near and wants to fill us. We pray of necessity because without God we are rootless and alone, and our lives lack depth. We pray in awe because God is the creator and we are creatures, the work of God's hands.

Two outstanding twentieth-century Christians, both converts to the faith from nonreligious backgrounds, tell how they were drawn to Catholic Christianity by the simple example of others kneeling quietly in prayer. In his famous autobiography, *The Seven Storey Mountain,* Thomas Merton describes the first time that he attended Mass. Slipping into a pew in the unfamiliar church, he noticed near him a young girl, perhaps sixteen years old, kneeling quietly in prayer. He writes, "I was very much impressed to see that someone who was young and beautiful could with such simplicity make prayer the real and serious and principle reason for going to church."[12] What this girl's example said to Merton was that God was not distant, but very near to us.

Edith Stein, the Jewish philosopher who became a Carmelite nun and died at Auschwitz, says something very similar. She describes pausing on a journey to Freiburg to visit the cathedral in Frankfurt am Main. There she saw a woman come into the almost empty church, enter a pew, and kneel quietly there. Later she wrote that she never forgot that moment, for it was something she had not experienced in synagogues or Protestant churches, where prayer seemed to be limited to worship. Here someone had come into an empty church, "as though to an intimate conversation."

This is what prayer is, a simple, intimate conversation with the God who loves us.

The Prayer of Jesus

The Gospels present Jesus as a man of prayer. He followed the religious traditions of his people, participating regularly in their official Sabbath worship "as was his custom" (Luke 4:16) and most probably reciting three times daily the *Shema,* the creedal prayer which begins "Hear, O Israel: the LORD is our God, the LORD alone" (cf. Deut 6:4–5). Luke especially stresses Jesus at prayer; his experience at the Jordan after his baptism takes place while he was praying (3:21). He shows Jesus praying before other important moments in his own life (5:16; 6:12; 9:18; 9:28; 11:1; 22:42; 23:46) and counseling others to pray (11:5–13; 18:1; 18:9–14; 21:36; 22:40). One beautiful saying of Jesus encourages the disciples to persevere in prayer; it is a lesson for us as well: "Ask, and it will be given you; search, and you will find; knock, and the door will be opened for you" (Luke 11:9).

Perhaps what is most suggestive of Jesus' relationship with God is the familiar term that he used in his own prayer, addressing God as "Abba," a family word that means not just the more formal "father," but something like "loving father." It was the kind of word a son or daughter would use within the intimacy of the family. No Jew at that time would have dared to address God in such familiar terms; indeed, devout Jews would not even pronounce God's holy name; they would always use some circumlocution such as "the Blessed One" (Mark 14:61). But the fact that Jesus regularly spoke to God in such familiar fashion suggests to us a great deal, not just about his own experience of God, but about the nature of prayer as well. Prayer is simply speaking in an intimate way with the God who loves and cares for each of us.

Perhaps the prayer of Jesus is best symbolized by the story of the agony in the garden. Here Jesus, knowing that he was about to fall into the hands of those who sought his life, prays simply, "Father, if you are willing, remove this cup from me; yet, not my will but yours be done" (Luke 22:42).

Reflection Questions

1. What role does prayer play in my life at present?

2. What prayer experiences have been significant for me in the past?

3. What would I like to bring to prayer during this retreat?

RECOGNIZING GOD'S PRESENCE

Ephesians 5:19–21

The story of Jesus dismissing his disciples and withdrawing into the hills after the miracle of the loaves has always fascinated me; according to Mark and Matthew he went there to pray (Mark 6:46; Matt 14:23; see also John 6:15). It's difficult to enter "into the mind" of Jesus, given the nature of the sources, but it is certainly possible that the miracle of the loaves was not just for the disciples, but perhaps even more for Jesus—an experience of God, a moment in which the Father's presence in his life became so clear, so evident.

We have all had such moments, moments when we've experienced God's presence in our ministry in a powerful way, and we've had to pull back a bit in prayer to reflect and consider, to give thanks and adore. These are moments of special grace in our lives, moments that can sustain us in more difficult times. In the words of Thomas Merton, "As soon as there is any reasonable indication that God is drawing the spirit into this way of contemplation, we ought to remain at peace in a prayer that is utterly simplified, stripped of acts and reflections and clean of images, waiting in emptiness and vigilant expectancy for the will of God to be done in us."[13]

Signs of God's Presence

What are the signs of God's presence in our lives? How do we recognize when God has been there? For St. Paul, one sign of grace seems to have been freedom. He speaks so often of freedom, using the beautiful expression, the "freedom of the glory of the children of God" (Rom 8:21), telling us that in the grace of Christ we have been freed—from the law, from sin, from death itself, and from eternal death. This emphasis on freedom needs to be understood in terms of Paul's own conversion experience: the transformation of the self-righteous Pharisee; this man who sought to justify himself and obtain his own righteousness through his observance of the law. In his quest he exacted the maximum penalty from other Jews who had a different religious experience from his own. There was much of the religious fanatic in Paul prior to his conversion, and he never forgot how God in Christ had set him free.

With his profound appreciation of the presence of the Spirit in the life of the Christian and the Christian community, he points to various signs of the Spirit. Faith, confessing Jesus as Lord testifies to the Spirit's presence (1 Cor 12:3). The charismata or spiritual gifts are a manifestation of the Spirit's presence (1 Cor 12:7).

Another sign is to be found in an ordered interior life. Thus he contrasts the works of the flesh—"fornication, impurity, licentiousness, idolatry, sorcery, enmities, strife, jealousy, anger, quarrels, dissensions, factions, envy, drunkenness, carousing, and things like these"—with the fruit of the Spirit, "love, joy, peace, patience, kindness, generosity, faithfulness, gentleness, and self-control" (Gal 5:19–21, 22–23).

In the Johannine tradition, with its source in the one called the Beloved Disciple, love is a preeminent sign of God's presence. John continually emphasizes the divine initiative: that God has first loved us and that he sent his Son to reveal his love; the Son who gives his life that we might have eternal life and might share in the divine life through the divine indwelling.

John speaks repeatedly of God dwelling as Father, Son, and Spirit in the believer; he uses over and over again the verb *menein*, "to remain with," "abide in," to express this mystery: "God is love, and those who abide in love abide in God, and God abides in them" (1 John 4:16).

For John, God's love is dynamic. The love that is God is revealed in Jesus, perfected in the lives of the disciples, and through their ministry draws the world back to God. We could say that John has a sacramental view of the Church; it is the sacrament of God's love for the world, and therefore must be itself a community of love if it is to bring others to the mystery of God. How tragic, then, if the Church fails to realize this vision of a community perfected in love.

Prayer of Personal Reminiscence

Like the disciples on the road to Emmaus, we sometimes only recognize the Lord's presence after he has gone. The prayer of personal reminiscence is a way of reflecting prayerfully over our life, to discern again where the Lord has been present, where he has touched us or manifested himself. There are many ways to make this prayer. We can consider different stages in our lives: earliest memories, childhood, teenage years, young adulthood, and important milestones. We can review different places where we have lived or gone to school, different stages in our careers, significant relationships, transitions, and new beginnings. What is important is bringing to mind in gratitude the different ways in which God has been present in all those persons, events, and situations that have shaped each of us to be the person we are today.

Reflection Questions

1. Where do I discern the Lord's mysterious presence at this particular moment in my life as I begin my retreat?

2. What are the signs of God's presence in my life?

Notes: Day One

1. Rudolf Otto, *The Idea of the Holy* (New York: Oxford University Press, 1958).

2. Edward Collins Vacek, "The Eclipse of Love for God," *America* 174 (March 19, 1996): 13.

3. Robert Wuthnow, *All in Sync: How Music and Art Are Revitalizing American Religion* (Berkeley: University of California Press, 2003), 24–25.

4. Thomas Merton, *New Seeds of Contemplation* (New York: New Directions Books, 1972), 82.

5. Vacek, p. 13.

6. Raymond Hedin, *Married to the Church* (Bloomington: Indiana University Press, 1995), 88.

7. Ibid., p. 88.

8. Ibid., p. 89.

9. Joseph Bernardin, "Priests: Religious Leaders, Doctors of the Soul," *Origins* 25 (May 25, 1995): 26.

10. Tertullian, *On Prayer,* cap. 29.

11. Henri J. Nouwen, *With Open Hands* (Notre Dame, IN: Ave Maria Press, 1972), 17.

12. Thomas Merton, *The Seven Storey Mountain* (New York: Harcourt Brace, 1976), 207–8.

13. Merton, *New Seeds of Contemplation,* p. 240.

DAY 2

THE TEMPTATIONS OF JESUS

Luke 4:1–13

A number of years ago when I was living in one of the student resident halls on campus, I went with my student resident advisors down to Mexico for a team building weekend, a kind of retreat together. We had a little cabin on the beach at Rosarito, a lovely place on a deserted bay in Baja California. After the noise of the dorm, where one gets use to the hearing five stereos blasting simultaneously, the quiet and solitude of the beach was welcoming.

But as we began unpacking, one of the students turned on a radio, cranked the volume so that the house was filled with the scratchy music of a distant station. The radio stayed on for most of the weekend, violating the quiet of the place. And I found myself wondering, what it is about us, particularly those of us who are younger, that makes us so uncomfortable with silence? Many seem almost afraid of it. Why do we have to surround ourselves with so much noise?

Going into the Desert

The gospel story of the temptations of Jesus takes place in the desert. In religious literature, the desert is an important symbol. The word suggests dryness, spaciousness, and solitude. It is a barren and elemental place, isolated and unforgiving, exposed to the forces of nature that beat down on the unprotected earth. The desert is a hostile environment, but there is also a profound peace there that can quiet and center those who venture into its solitude.

In the Bible the desert is the place for the encounter with God. Stripped of distractions and open to the infinite mystery of the universe sensed in the sun, the wind, the alternating heat and cold, and the vast expanse of the stars, the man or woman in the desert stands naked and alone before God. Moses, Elijah, John the Baptist, Jesus, Paul all had desert experiences in which they found themselves in God's mysterious presence. The monastic movement that continues to enrich the Church had its beginnings in the deserts of Egypt, and some religious communities today require their younger members to spend time there alone.

How will you encounter God during this retreat? Sometimes God can be found in silent awe and adoration; sometimes in that profound inner longing that comes from our deepest desires; sometimes in the awareness of a deep peace that witnesses to God's presence within us.

However, one cannot encounter God without also coming face to face with one's self, and so the desert is also an arena for the struggle with the evil spirits, the demonic powers that contend for control of the human spirit. Athanasius's *Life of Antony,* the story St. Antony of Egypt, the father of monasticism, tells of his being confronted by the devil in his desert cell. Appearing under various disguises, the devil sought to turn him from his purpose, filling his imagination with sensual images and arousing him with sexual feelings. The desert then is also a place of testing and purification.

After his baptism and revelatory experience at the Jordan, Jesus withdrew into the desert for a period of prayer and fasting, and during that time he was temped by the devil. It was only after this period of personal struggle that he began his own public ministry.

We can presuppose that the temptations as they are presented in Matthew 4:1–11 and Luke 4:1–13 are more symbolic than historical, but they represent what must have been real temptations in the life of Jesus. We need to take the humanity of Jesus seriously; he was like us in all things, except sin, and that includes temptations similar to those that emerge from our inner struggles and the possibilities that life puts before us. What are the temptations that Jesus faced in the Synoptic stories?

The First Temptation: Putting One's Own Needs First

The first temptation arises out of Jesus' hunger; he has been fasting and is hungry. Approaching him, the devil said to him: "If you are the Son of God, command this stone to become a loaf of bread" (Luke 4:3).

Jesus rejects the temptation, saying: "One does not live by bread alone." But his hunger is not just physical; like us, he has hungers that come from his social and psychological nature: a hunger for companionship, human closeness, intimacy, success, a good reputation. He had genuine human needs, just as each of us has. The temptation is to put his needs before his mission, putting himself first, using his powers or gifts to take care of his own needs rather than continuing his search for God through prayer and watching.

The Second Temptation:
The Seduction of Power

Then the devil led him up and showed him in an instant all the kingdoms of the world. And the devil said to him, "To you I will give their glory and all this authority; for it has been given over to me, and I give it to anyone I please. If you, then, will worship me, it will all be yours." (Luke 4:5–7)

The second temptation appeals subtly to Jesus' sense of mission; it is the temptation to use his power for the sake of his ministry. It seems like something good, but means actually to make a god of success. Perhaps one of the most difficult struggles for Jesus in his ministry was his inability to accomplish what he wanted by the shear force of his will. He could not compel others to accept his message. He could not change their hearts. He was not able to accomplish all that he wanted. Think of the picture of Jesus weeping over Jerusalem, seeing its future and the failure of his own mission (Luke 19:41–44). But he would not seek to win them over through the illegitimate use of power or the worship of false gods. He could only speak to their hearts.

And there were others working against him, people whose blindness to their own narrow self-interests resulted in an implacable hostility toward him and his mission. Ultimately they conspired with the Roman government officials in order to get rid of him. In a very real sense, the evil present in the world, the evil that is the result of human sinfulness, took on concrete expression in these political and religious leaders who refused to recognize the presence of God in his ministry. He must have been tempted to seek and use power for the sake of his mission, but that would have been contrary to the Father's way.

All he could do was to invite them, share with them his vision of God's kingdom, appealing to their best instincts. But he would not violate their freedom. There is a basic principle of the spiritual life here: God always respects our freedom, never compels us, not even for our own good.

The Third Temptation: Manipulating Others

> Then the devil took him to Jerusalem, and placed him on the pinnacle of the temple, saying to him, "If you are the Son of God, throw yourself down from here, for it is written, 'He will command his angels concerning you, to protect you,' and 'On their hands they will bear you up, so that you will not dash your foot against a stone.'" (Luke 4:9–11)

This temptation also builds on Jesus' desire to succeed, to win others over to his vision of God's reign. The devil's temptation is to dazzle others with his power, which really means to manipulate or con them, to take away their freedom. But Jesus resists this one too, dismissing the devil with "Do not put the Lord your God to the test."

There is considerable insight in these temptation stories. They are temptations for Jesus, for the Church, and all those in ministry. But they are temptations, not to obvious evil, but to a lesser good. The temptations are to use his powers for the sake of his mission. People growing in their spiritual life and discipleship usually experience this kind of temptation. They want to be faithful, to do what is right. They would reject the temptation to obvious evil.

We often experience this ourselves. We want to be successful, to bring others around to our point of view, to control how they think. We easily identify our work with the Lord's. We want to be happy, to satisfy our hungers, to take care of our legitimate needs, to take charge of our destinies rather than imitate Jesus' total trust and abandonment to God. We often face these temptations in the desert, as Jesus did. Not a bad place to begin a retreat.

Reflection Questions

1. What are the temptations most detrimental to my ministry?

2. In what ways do I put my own needs first?

3. To what "lesser goods" or false gods do I find myself drawn?

THE FALSE SELF

Genesis 3

Each of the temptations Jesus experiences in the desert represents a rejection of the truth of who he is. Rather than living as the Son of a loving father, nourished by God's word, worshipping and serving God alone, trusting completely in God, Jesus is tempted to reject his own humanity as a child of God. He is tempted to become someone else, to use his gifts to benefit himself, to play the magician, to have power over others. In other words, Jesus was wrestling with what we call today the false self, the temptation to be someone other than the unique person God created him to be.

The false self has a thousand faces. It is the autonomous self, the self-sufficient individual, the sovereign ego. It is the person in the mask, the one who hides behind the façade, the public persona who can't afford to let the real self emerge. It is the one who succumbs to the temptation of the serpent in the Garden, to eat the forbidden fruit and become like God (cf. Gen 3:5).

Each of us is tempted to buy into some false self; to try and be the person who everyone likes, who knows all the answers, who is always in control, or the person around whom the world revolves. These false selves are often the shields we erect around ourselves as we recover from childhood wounds, some secret violence done to us, the sinfulness in our environments, and tragedies in our personal histories. They are coping mechanisms for dealing with a sinful world, a world damaged and scarred by original sin. We seek to protect ourselves by keeping others at a distance.

James Carroll's book, *An American Requiem: God, My Father, and the War that Came Between Us,*[1] is a good example of a man struggling to find his true self. The son of an Air Force general who advised presidents and was the confidant of cardinals, Carroll was deeply influenced by his father's desire to have a son become a priest. He became a Paulist. Early in his priesthood, he began to struggle and protest against the growing U.S. involvement in Vietnam, even as his father in the Pentagon worked to promote it. The book is the story of his effort to find himself against the triple authority figures of father, Church, and country that dominated his life. Ultimately he left the priesthood to become the writer that his Paulist brethren sensed he would one day be.

One can choose ministry or priesthood for the wrong reasons. Usually those people should leave to discover their true selves. But it is equally true that one can leave for the wrong reasons, and that the new self that beckons may represent one more attempt to avoid the mysterious call of God.

The True Self

One meets one's true self in the desert of contemplative prayer. This is one of the great lessons we can learn from Thomas Merton. In his *New Seeds of Contemplation* he wrote, "For me to be a saint means to be myself. Therefore the problem of sanctity and salvation is in fact the problem of finding out who I am and of discovering my true self."[2] Contemplation could never be a way of avoiding reality; it was always a struggle to get at the reality of things, to see them as they really are.

Merton saw contemplation as a deepening of faith to the point where the union with God that is already given in our very nature breaks into our experience. It is not the result of some psychological trick, nor is it the result of special methods or techniques; contemplation is a genuine grace, something that comes as a gift. In his poetic language, Merton describes it as a door opening in the center of our being through which we seem to fall into an immense depth of silence and presence while our ordinary powers of thinking and imagining are stilled.

What happens in contemplation is that the real or inner self begins to awaken, the true self that is free and spontaneous and that manifests itself only in silence and humility, in purity of heart and indifference.[3] The inner self is far different from the persona or ego: "It is a great mistake" Merton writes, "to confuse the *person* (the spiritual and hidden self, united with God), and the *ego*, the exterior, empirical self, the psychological individuality who forms a kind of mask for the inner and hidden self."[4]

There is a wonderful passage in *Conjectures of a Guilty Bystander* where Merton describes the awakening of the birds in the valley that surrounds his monastery. From the darkness and silence of the night, God opens their eyes with the dawn, and they begin to speak to him; "Then, they one by one wake up, and become birds. They manifest themselves as birds, beginning to sing. Presently they will be fully themselves, and will even fly."[5] These birds are fully themselves, their real selves; they are what God has created them to be.

The Jesuit poet Gerard Manley Hopkins says something very similar in his great poem, "As Kingfishers Catch Fire," turning nouns into verbs to carry his meaning:

> ...the just man justices;
> Keeps grace: that keeps all his goings graces;
> Acts in God's eye what in God's eye he is—
> Christ.

In Hopkins's poem there is no mask, no false self, no separation between how the just man acts and what he truly is; to paraphrase, thè just man acts justly, acts as the Christ God's grace makes him to be. Would that we could so easily discover our true selves, be who we are in God's eyes, wake up singing like the birds, acting justly like the just man who "justices." For Merton, this is what contemplatives mean when they speak of the inner self: "Since our inmost 'I' is the perfect image of God, then when that 'I' awakens, he finds within himself the Presence of Him Whose image he is."[6]

For Merton, with his great love of nature, any natural vista wherein the immensity and mysterious presence of the divine are suggested could draw one into contemplation: "The sweep and serenity of a landscape, fields and hills, are enough to keep a contemplative riding the quiet interior tide of his peace and desire for hours at a time"[7]

Merton did not often discuss his own personal experience in prayer. But there is one often quoted passage, contained in a letter to the Sufi scholar Aziz Abdul that to a certain extent lifts the veil of his reticence:

> Strictly speaking I have a very simple way of prayer. It is centered entirely on attention to the presence of God and to His will and His love. That is to say that it is centered on *faith* by which alone we can know the presence of God....Yet it does not mean imagining anything or conceiving a precise image of God, for to my mind this would be a kind of idolatry.[8]

A retreat often brings about a confrontation with our false self, but we shouldn't be surprised if we experience some temptations in the process. We are not of much interest to the evil spirit while the false self is still in place. But the "enemy of our nature" gets very nervous as our true nature begins to emerge— the inner self alive with the mysterious presence of God.

Reflection Questions

1. How does God see me as I begin my retreat?
2. What blocks the emergence of my true self?
3. What intimations do I have of my true self?

THE INCARNATION

Matthew 1:18–25

The second week of the *Spiritual Exercises* begins with a wonderful meditation on the incarnation. Ignatius asks the retreatant to imagine the Trinity looking down from the heavens on human beings in all their misery:

Here I recall how the Three Divine Persons gazed upon the vast sweep of the earth, around the whole globe, fully peopled. I recall how, watching the multitude sinking down into Hell, they make the decision deep in eternity that the Second Person should become human in order to save the human race. And so, when the fullness of time came, the Divine Persons sent the holy angel Gabriel to Our Lady.

I see the peoples of earth in all their diversity of costume and mores. Some are light-skinned and some are dark-skinned; some at peace and others warring; some weeping and others laughing; some healthy and others sick; some are being born and others are dying; and so on.

The first point is to see the persons on either side. I see and ponder over the Three Divine Persons on their royal dais or seated on the throne of Divine Majesty. They gaze upon the full sweep and circle of earth and see how all the peoples, living in such blindness, die and go down into hell.

The second point is to listen to what individuals are saying all around this world, that is, how they talk with each other, how they swear and blaspheme, and so on. Likewise, I hear what the three Divine Persons are saying, which is, "Let us work out the redemption of the human race," and so on.

The third point is to watch what the people all around the world are doing, that is, wounding, killing, going down to Hell. Likewise, what the Divine Persons are doing, that is, working out the most holy Incarnation and the rest. And in the same way, what the angel and Our Lady are doing, that is, the angel carrying out his office of ambassador and Our Lady humbling herself and giving thanks to the Divine Majesty (nos. 102–8).[9]

This meditation on the incarnation is almost child-like in its simple, imaginative quality, and yet it is very profound. What it shows us is the infinite compassion of God who beholds the human race in all its beauty, but sees also its folly, blindness, and violence. This God is not distant from us. This is a God who is close to his people, a God who hears the cry of the poor (Exod 22:26), a God of compassion who chose to become one of us.

It would not take much to bring the meditation up to date, to remember the horrors that took place just so recently in Cambodia, Central America, Rwanda, Bosnia, or the Sudan; the victims such violence leaves in its wake, the millions of men, women, and children maimed by the land mines sown in their farms and fields; the cynical use of political power for personal enrichment in so many Third-World countries; the young people growing up without hope, now often armed with automatic weapons, like the children we've seen in our daily papers with Kalashnikovs. Recently in Uganda, children were kidnapped from their homes, the boys forced to commit acts of violence and murder against family members and peers to prevent them from returning home; the girls used as sex slaves.[10] In many countries the sex industry and poverty sell children into prostitution. Whole countries have been ravaged by AIDS.

Closer to home we can think of the casual disregard for the poor and the powerless; the violence in the ghettos of our inner cities; the children caught up in the culture of the gangs and drive-by shootings; lives wasted by drugs—crack for the poor, designer cocaine for the well to do; children in broken homes, growing up without fathers, or suffering physical or sexual abuse from relatives or other trusted adults, even from priests. We can think of the billions of dollars spent on weapons of war, the threat of terrorism, the pornography and abortion industries. It is in this context that we should understand Ignatius's words: "They make the decision deep in eternity that the Second Person should become human in order to save the human race."

The mystery of the incarnation is not just God's entering our world in a moment of time, although it is that as well. What the incarnation means is that God has joined himself irrevocably to us out of compassion and love, that God has become a part of our lives, and that God is present in the midst of all the tragedies of our world. The incarnation is happening now.

Contemporary thinkers often use the presence of so much suffering and evil in the world as an argument against the existence of God. So much suffering, particularly of the innocent, is an obstacle to belief. How could a good God create such a world; how could an all-powerful God permit such suffering? Why does God remain silent? The world's religions wrestled with this question after the devastating tsunami in south Asia on December 26, 2004, which killed over 200,000 people.

Although the mystery of suffering can never be adequately understood, we have to be cautious of our tendency to speak of God as omnipotent. Making God the author of every worldly event risks making God the author of evil as well. In some ways this is as naive as Ignatius's picture of the conversation among the Trinity we have been considering. As Pope John Paul II suggests in his best-selling little book, *Crossing the Threshold of Hope,* God's very creation of a universe of freedom can be understood as a self-limitation of the divine power. He writes, "in a certain sense one could say that *confronted with our human freedom, God decided to make Himself 'impotent.'*"[11] God cannot not respect our freedom.

Therefore, rather than seeing God as the immediate cause of every event, it makes more sense to image a long-suffering and compassionate God who sorrows with us and who is mysteriously at work bringing good out of evil, victory out of defeat, life out of death. Nowhere is this shown more clearly than in the life of Jesus, especially in his death and resurrection.

Reflection Questions

1. Where have I experienced personally the desperate plight of the poor and the powerless?

2. Where is the word of God becoming incarnate for me today?

Notes: Day Two

1. James Carroll, *An American Requiem: God, My Father, and the War that Came Between Us* (Boston: Houghton Mifflin, 1996).

2. Thomas Merton, *New Seeds of Contemplation* (New York: New Directions Books, 1972), 31.

3. Lawrence S. Cunningham, ed., "The Inner Experience," in *Thomas Merton: Spiritual Master* (Mahwah, NJ: Paulist Press, 1992), 297–302.

4. Merton, *New Seeds of Contemplation,* 279.

5. Thomas Merton, *Conjectures of a Guilty Bystander* (Garden City, NY: Doubleday, 1966), 117.

6. "The Inner Experience," in *Thomas Merton: Spiritual Master,* 309.

7. Merton, *New Seeds of Contemplation,* 242–43.

8. William H. Shannon, ed., *The Hidden Ground of Love: Letters by Thomas Merton on Religious Experience and Social Concerns* (New York: Farrar, Straus, 1985), 64.

9. Joseph A. Tetlow, trans., *Ignatius Loyola: Spiritual Exercises* (New York: Crossroad, 1992), 100–101.

10. See http://www.invisiblechildren.com/.

11. John Paul II, *Crossing the Threshold of Hope,* ed. Vittorio Messori (New York: Random House, 1994), 61.

DAY 3

THE BAPTISM OF JESUS

Luke 3:21–22

The story of Jesus begins with his baptism. We know almost nothing about his life before that moment, though the fascination of some early Christians with the idea of the Son of God as a child has filled the apocryphal gospels with pious stories of his youth. We too would like to pierce the veil of time and history to know the details of Jesus' life more completely, to see the ways in which his story is like our own.

We know that Jesus lived his young adult years as a carpenter (Mark 6:3) in his home village of Nazareth, and that at some point, he left home, mother, and friends and traveled some ninety miles south to Judea where John was baptizing. Most likely he had heard reports that a new prophet had appeared in the land and wanted to hear his message.

We do not know the exact details of what happened at the Jordan. The earliest Gospel, Mark, simply announces that Jesus was baptized by John. Luke, sensitive to the place of prayer in Jesus' life, situates his baptism within the context of his religious experience: "When all the people were baptized, and when Jesus also had been baptized and was praying, the heaven was opened, and the Holy Spirit descended upon him in bodily form like a dove. And a voice came from heaven, 'You are my Son, the Beloved; with you I am well pleased'" (Luke 3:21–22).

Some of the later evangelists seem uncomfortable with this picture of Jesus, the sinless one, submitting to John's baptism, which was a sign of repentance. Matthew inserts a phrase in which John protests that he should be baptized by Jesus, and John, the last evangelist, never actually mentions the baptism itself, only the revelatory vision. But certainly Jesus would have been aware of himself as part of a sinful people, Israel, whose coming judgment John proclaimed, and no doubt came forward as a sign of his own openness to whatever God was about to do.

Whatever happened, the experience changed his life, for Jesus did not return to his village and work. Instead he seems to have become one of the Baptist's followers for a while. His first disciples came from John's group and Jesus and his disciples also baptized in the early days of his ministry according to the fourth evangelist (John 3:22).[1] There are a number of important similarities between John's preaching and that of Jesus: both called people to a conversion of mind and heart, there was a note of urgency in the preaching of both as well as an eschatological dimension, and Jesus also gathered disciples about him.

At some point, however, Jesus parted from John and moved off to begin his own ministry. The differences in their preaching are evident. John's message was a stern one about God's coming judgment, filled with images of fire and axe, cutting down and winnowing, warning the people that Jewish descent was of no account and calling them to a repentance that would be expressed in deeds (Luke 3:7–9; cf. Matt 3:7–10). And he warned them of a greater one coming, one whose sandal strap he was not worthy to unfasten.

Jesus' message was different. Although it included the call to conversion, it was the genuinely joyful news of the reign of God being at hand; it was good news for the poor. He healed the sick, freed others from evil spirits, and proclaimed the forgiveness of sins. Whereas John's lifestyle was ascetical, Jesus' practice of table fellowship with those marginalized by the religious community led to the accusation, frequently made, that he was a glutton and drunkard, a friend of tax collectors and sinners (Luke 7:34; cf. Mark 2:16). We can only conclude that his own religious experience was different from that of John. Indeed, John seems to have had doubts about Jesus and his itinerant ministry as he sent some of his disciples to inquire if he was truly the one to come (Luke 7:20; Matt 11:3). We have no way of knowing if his doubts were ever resolved.

Thus, Jesus' baptism by John marked a turning point in his life. John himself played an important role. Perhaps it was an experience as well of special intimacy with the one he would call "Abba," something without precedent for a Jew of his time.

Reflecting on our Call

We might use the story of the baptism of Jesus to reflect on the mystery of our own call, our memories of the beginnings of our own vocation. Perhaps what drew us was the desire for the holy, for God, and that desire is still present, though often deeply buried beneath the routines and distractions that make up our lives. We desire to experience the living God, the one who called us and whose mysterious presence in our lives still draws us forward.

We need to return to our foundational experience of being called, to the moment when we first experienced our vocations. Perhaps there was a dramatic instance in our life that began a movement in a new direction. Often teachers or friends played an important role, providing models of people of faith. Or maybe the Lord entered our lives at a moment when we were least prepared, when we were not expecting his coming. It might be helpful to begin by asking, when did I first become aware of God?

What drew me to what must remain always a mystery? Who were the models and mentors for me?

Was I seeking God? When did God first become real for me? Did I sense myself drawn toward the holy? Thomas Merton says in his autobiography, *The Seven Storey Mountain,* that when he was a child he had an irresistible urge to worship the pilot light in the stove in his mother's kitchen. It suggested for him something mysterious, the other, the holy. Some of us have had similar experiences.

Sometimes a passage of scripture can speak to us powerfully, becoming in a whole new sense God's word. I remember years ago trying to discern if God was truly calling me to the priesthood. I had many doubts, fears, and hesitations. One morning at a weekday Mass, following the Latin of the liturgy in my *St. Andrew's Missal,* the words of the communion verse suddenly struck home:

> You did not choose me
> But I chose you.
> And I appointed you
> to go and bear fruit,
> fruit that will last. (John 15:16)

Those words seemed addressed to me personally; the moment was one of clarity, a special grace that I have never forgotten.

Reflection Questions

1. How did I first experience the holy?

2. Did my image of God come from my parents or from the depths of my own personality?

3. How would I tell the story of discovering my own vocation?

JESUS THE COMPASSION OF GOD

Mark 1:40–45

Jesus himself is the embodiment of the compassion of God; God among us in the flesh. His ministry is a ministry of compassion. The Gospels frequently show Jesus acting out of compassion, and use words that indicate that he was deeply moved by the suffering he encountered.

Mark's language says this vividly. He says that upon meeting a leper Jesus was "moved with pity," or better, "compassion," which suggests in English "to suffer with." He uses the Greek *embrimesamenos,* which denotes strong emotions, emotions that boil over and find expression in groaning (Mark 1:43). In the story of the miracle of the loaves, he tells us again that Jesus was moved with pity when he saw the vast crowd of people, "like sheep without a shepherd" (Mark 6:34). Here he uses a form of the verb *splagchnizomai,* which means literally, to feel something in one's bowels, hence, "compassion." The same verb appears in Luke 7:13, when Jesus meets the widow of Nain accompanying her only son to his burial; again Jesus is described as being "moved with pity" (NAB).

These passages suggest that Jesus' own heart was deeply moved when he witnessed the sufferings of others, that their pain became his own, that he groaned within. Do we have hearts like his? Or do we experience our own hearts as hard, unmoved, lacking in compassion? We have so many excuses.

Jesus showed himself to be the compassion of God because he was able to see others as they really were. His outlook was contemplative. He did not stereotype as we so often do. He did not see just a "widow" on her way to a funeral, but a mother grieving for her son and facing a future alone, without support. We categorize and name the other as a "beggar" or "alcoholic" or "former priest" or "fallen-away Catholic" rather than recognizing him or her as a person like ourselves, struggling with weakness and temptations, with broken dreams and personal tragedies. We can't be compassionate to a stereotype, but we can to a person, another human being with a name and a personal history.

So often our own outlook, deeply influenced by our culture, is instrumentalist. We look on persons and things in terms of what they can do for us, as the means to some end. So the CEO of a major corporation can lay off fifteen thousand employees because the company needed to "down-size" and the stock holders expect their dividends. Or we can justify some disordered relationship because "it's only human," or because we need the support, or because it doesn't do anyone any harm. Or we dismiss some one on our staff because we see him or her as a threat.

Elizabeth Johnson speaks of Jesus' compassionate service as a way of "enacting" the reign of God. He called others to follow him as disciples; he showed a special concern for the marginal people of his society, seeking out those suffering physically, spiritually, and socially, including them in his table fellowship, showing them that love was at the heart of the reign of God. He healed the sick, drove out evil spirits, proclaimed the forgiveness of sins, restoring *shalom* to all.[2]

Jesus is able to reach out to others in compassion because he doesn't seek anything for himself. St. Paul uses an early Christian hymn to describe the incarnation of Jesus as a *kenosis,* a self-emptying: "though he was in the form of God, did not regard equality with God as something to be exploited, but emptied himself, taking the form of a slave, being born in human like-ness" (Phil 2:6–7).

Our own ministry, if it is to mediate to others the mysteri-ous presence of God, must be rooted in the compassion of Jesus who emptied himself for our sakes. We need to see others as he did, we should ask for the grace to have what St. Paul calls the mind of Christ (1 Cor 2:16). Thus in the second week of the Exercises, St. Ignatius encourages the retreatant to pray for that interior knowledge of Christ our Lord who has become man for me, that I may more love and follow him.

Reflection Questions

1. Where has the compassion of Jesus become real for me?

2. Where do the sorrows of contemporary men and women most touch my life?

3. Where have I acted with compassion?

HOSPITALITY AND TABLE FELLOWSHIP

Luke 7:36–50

Some years ago I spent a sabbatical semester at the Institute for Ecumenical and Intercultural Research on the campus of St. John's Abbey and University at Collegeville, Minnesota. It was the first time that I as a Jesuit had spent an extended period of time in a community that was Benedictine in spirit and orientation, and I was particularly impressed with the community's spirit of hospitality. Hospitality is very much part of the Benedictine charism, rooted in the Rule of St. Benedict:

> All guests who present themselves are to be welcomed as Christ, for he himself will say: "I was a stranger and you welcomed me..." (Matt 25:35). Once a guest has been announced, the superior and the brothers are to meet him with all the courtesy of love. All humility should be shown in addressing a guest on arrival and departure. By a bow or by a complete prostration of the body, Christ is to be adored because he is indeed welcomed in them....Great care and concern are to be shown in receiving poor people and pilgrims, because in them more particularly is Christ received.[3]

There was something very gracious about the way the Benedictines at Collegeville practiced hospitality. Their style is quiet, low keyed. You have to get to know them. They don't push themselves forward. They have developed a way of life and liturgical style that brings together marvelously both monastic community and inclusivity. The whole environment at Collegeville bespeaks a welcome.

The church is always open. There are pamphlets to welcome guests and help them find their way around. The liturgical space invites participation. The monastic choir is arranged in a semicircle around the altar; while there is space reserved for the monastic community, the guests are also welcome to participate in the Eucharist and the Liturgy of the Hours from the stalls. Newcomers find a monk waiting to help them find their way in using the various books for the office—all eight of them! When I first arrived I was helped by one elderly monk who I later discovered was the great Father Godfrey Diekmann, then in his eighties. Living on campus you gradually get to know some of the monks, and I didn't meet one that wasn't gracious. They would go out of their way to make you feel welcome. They have a wonderful way of letting you know who they are in a nonintrusive way, without making you feel that you are different or don't belong. The effect of their spirit of hospitality was so strong that I found myself reflecting on it and praying for that grace.

Hospitality is the sign of a gracious spirit. It is deeply rooted in the biblical tradition. The Old Testament speaks frequently of welcoming and caring for the widow, the orphan, the stranger in the land (cf. Exod 22:20–21). In welcoming the three strangers at Mamre, Abraham welcomed God (Gen 18:1–15), and was blessed for it. St. Paul wrote, "Welcome one another, therefore, as Christ has welcomed you, for the glory of God" (Rom 15:7). In a world with so much poverty and political oppression, more developed countries are challenged in a particular way to welcome the stranger, and to resist laws that scapegoat or penalize immigrants.

Table Fellowship

In the ancient Near East, table fellowship was particularly important as a sign of welcome and communion. Even today, Muslims consider sharing meals an important part of their life and spirituality. Since food is one of God's gifts, sharing with others, even eating from the same plate, marks Muslims as belonging to one family, symbolizing and deepening their relationships.

Jesus exemplified hospitality in his ministry, particularly in his tradition of table fellowship, the foundation on which our Eucharist is based. It is fascinating to reflect on how much of Jesus' ministry took place at table. He shared joyous meals with his disciples, at which the very idea of fasting seemed somehow inappropriate (Mark 3:18–19). He went to meals in the homes of the religious leaders of the people, like the story of his meal in the home of Simon the Pharisee, the meal interrupted by the woman who came and washed the feet of Jesus with her tears (Luke 7:36–50). He shared meals with the religious outcasts of his day, the "tax collectors and sinners," for which he was so frequently criticized (Mark 2:16; Luke 7:34). He provided meals for the multitude, joyous meals of bread and fish that foreshadowed the fullness of the great eschatological banquet in the kingdom (Mark 6:34–44; cf. Isa 25:6–8).

On the night before he died, he shared one last meal with the disciples he loved and had so often instructed at table; this "last supper" took on new meaning when he spoke of his own death on their behalf, identifying the bread and wine with his body and blood.

What is so clear is the inclusive nature of Jesus' table fellowship; no one was excluded from his company or from a share in the reign of God he proclaimed. But the spirit of our age, in spite of all our talk about celebrating diversity and multiculturalism, is too often one of exclusivity.

How tragic, if the Church that continues Jesus' ministry, is not seen as a place of hospitality. As Cardinal Roger Mahony of Los Angeles said in his 1997 pastoral on the liturgy, "The Sunday assembly…should be the one experience in our lives when we will not be sorted out by education level, skin color, intelligence, politics, sexual orientation, wealth or lack of it, or any other human condition."[4]

But many today do not experience the Church as welcoming—among them, the poor and less educated, divorced and remarried people, singles, gays and lesbians, women, youth—all with their own gifts to bring to the service of God's people. How often have we met alienated Catholics who have felt turned away, not welcome, or have simply stopped participating because of the harshness of some priest or minister?

Priests carry on Jesus' ministry of table fellowship in a special way by presiding at the Eucharist. It is very possible that the role of eucharistic presidency was linked with hospitality from the beginning, as the first Eucharists were held in homes, the house churches we know of from Paul's letters (Rom 16:5; 1 Cor 16:19; Col 4:15). The host or householder would welcome the community and perhaps preside at its sacred meal.

Particularly at the Eucharist, priests act *in persona Christi,* in the person of Christ. They need to ask themselves, can I welcome the stranger, the alien, and the outcast? Can I welcome those who resent me because of my position? Will others be able to see Christ Jesus in me when I preside? Will visitors in the congregation feel at home? Other ministers also might reflect on how they welcome those who seem less interested in their programs, those who are alienated from the Church, or those who attend infrequently.

What about the very difficult issue of intercommunion? Catholic and Protestant churches view the question of eucharistic hospitality very differently. For most Protestants, it is the Lord Jesus who invites baptized believers to his table, and they think no Church has the right to restrict it. They practice open communion. For the Catholic and Orthodox churches, eucharistic communion is a sign of full communion in life and faith, even though the *Decree on Ecumenism* recognizes that *communicatio in sacris* might sometimes be a means to unity (*Unitatis Redintegratio* 8).

The Eucharist presumes and celebrates inclusivity, our oneness in Christ. How can we be faithful to the tradition of our Church and still be hospitable and inclusive? Two extremes: One is the priest who takes it upon himself to invite all forward, violating the present discipline of his Church. The other is that of the zealot who polices the communion line so that only the canonically pure may participate. It is a very difficult and painful issue.

What about the destitute, the transients, the professional con men who call regularly at the rectory door? These calls are some of the most difficult. My own reaction too often is anger and a sense of being manipulated. Many of these visitors play on our guilt. I once gave $40.00 for an emergency trip of mercy to a man who told me an incredible story, complete with supporting documents and convincing letters of recommendation, only to realize the moment I handed him the money that I had been conned. Several days later I saw him downtown coming out of a bar. But among the manipulators and con artists there are other cases of desperate need. How will you deal with them?

All who minister in Jesus' name must practice a ministry of hospitality. Do we make the gay person feel welcome, or the gay or lesbian couple? What about those who are in second marriages without annulments? How to be welcoming to them and still be faithful to the Church we represent? How do we welcome youth, young adults, and singles in our family-oriented parishes? Do we welcome the poor and those in need?

Reflection Questions

1. When have I been moved by the grace of hospitality?

2. Where do I find it difficult to be inclusive?

3. Do I take the time to share meals with close friends?

THE WORKERS IN THE VINEYARD

Matthew 20:1–16

Matthew's parable of the workers in the vineyard is a challenging one over which to pray. Jesus compares the reign of God to the owner of an estate who goes out at dawn to hire workmen for his vineyard, agreeing to pay them the usual daily wage. Several times more he goes out finding other men standing around the marketplace who are not working, and he sends them into his vineyard, telling them he will pay them whatever is fair. Finally he goes out in the late afternoon and finds others still idle, because as they tell him, "no one has hired us." So he sends them also into his vineyard.

At the end of the day he calls the workers together, starting with those hired last, paying each one of them a day's wage. When those hired first come to be paid, they suppose that they'll be paid more, but they also receive each a day's wage. When they complain to the owner that they have born the heat of the day and therefore should be paid more than the latecomers, the owner responds, "Friend, I am doing you no wrong; did you not agree with me for the usual daily wage? Take what belongs to you and go; I choose to give to this last the same as I give to you. Am I not allowed to do what I choose with what belongs to me? Or are you envious because I am generous?" The parable ends, "So the last will be first, and the first will be last" (Matt 20:13–16).

For years I disliked this parable immensely; I thought it very unfair, going against my instinctive sense of what is right and just. Of course those who worked longer should be paid more. How could anything else be fair? Part of it was my own unconscious Pelagianism, my sense that we should get what we work for and earn what we get. But the parable is saying that God is not like us; God's ways are not our ways. God's goodness and generosity turns our own way of seeing things upside down, challenging our standards, forcing us out of our complacency and requiring a radically new vision. In New Testament terms, this calls for *metanoia*. There is something fundamentally unsettling about this.

Part of my discomfort might have been also occasioned by the reversal of status suggested by the last line, "the first shall be last and the last shall be first," the eschatological reversal that occurs so often in Jesus' parables. Think for a moment of parables like the good Samaritan (Luke 10:29–37), the rich man and Lazarus (Luke 16:19–35), the marriage feast (Matt 22:1–14), the parable of the talents (Matt 25:14–30), and the prodigal son (Luke 15:11–32), all of which suggest a new way of imagining God and God's ways. In the words of Eamonn Bredin there is something shocking and subversive about the parables of Jesus: "It is the *Samaritan* who is neighbor, it the *last* who are first, it is the *lost* who are rejoiced over, the *stranger* who is at table, the *wastrel* son who is embraced and fêted."[5] This is not easy to hear.

The parable of the workers brings into focus God's special concern for the poor and the powerless that recurs so often in the prophets: the constant refrain to deal justly with the widow, the orphan, the stranger in the land. It is what is proclaimed about the coming of God's promised salvation in Mary's *Magnificat*:

> He has brought down the powerful
> from their thrones,
> and lifted up the lowly;

he has filled the hungry with
good things,
and sent the rich away empty. (Luke 1:52–53)

God's special concern for the poor is a basic theme in the preaching of Jesus, expressed so clearly in the Beatitudes (Matt 5:3–12; Luke 6:20–26). For it is the poor, the mourners, the hungry, the merciful, the peacemakers, those who hunger and thirst for justice who are called blessed in the kingdom of God. That the Beatitudes are at the center of the preaching of Jesus has not always been appreciated by Christians, though communities like Jean Vanier's *l'Arche* and the Catholic Worker communities in the United States have placed them at the center of their spirituality.

Finally, the parable reflects the daily struggles of real people in Jesus' time, particularly the disadvantaged. Recent studies have shed considerable light on Galilean social conditions; they provide the background to this parable. In Jesus' time the plight of the poor was worsening due to changes in the rural economy. Many small landowners, weakened by a triple tax structure, had lost their property or were reduced to subsistence farming often on barren land. The farming out of the right to collect taxes itself was open to corruption, as we know from the Gospels. Many people were in debt, while some were forced into slavery. "In such a situation parables about unlucky tenant farmers, day labors in vineyards, absentee landlords, unscrupulous middlemen and the like would hardly have sounded like pious platitudes. They would have run true to the realities of life, a social commentary on how the coming Dominion of God would ultimately change the situation."[6]

I didn't grasp the social dimensions of this parable fully until I began reflecting on the Mexican immigrant workers I always see standing in a long line outside a massive cut-rate building supply depot close to our university; these men are there, from early in the morning till late in the day, waiting like the men in the parable for someone to hire them. They are day labors desperate for a contractor to beckon them into his pick-up truck, to give them work for a few hours so that they can provide food and shelter for their families. The parable says that God is concerned for each of them, as we should be.

Reflection Questions

1. What parables do I find uncomfortable?

2. Where do I have regular contact with the disadvantaged?

Notes: Day Three

1. John P. Meier argues that this tradition is likely historical, even if a later editor feels a need to correct it. *A Marginal Jew: Rethinking the Historical Jesus, Vol. II* (New York: Doubleday, 1994), 118–22.

2. Elizabeth A. Johnson, *Consider Jesus: Waves of Renewal in Christology* (New York: Crossroad, 1990), 54–56.

3. Timothy Fry, ed., *Abridged Edition of the Rule of St. Benedict 1980* (Collegeville, MN: The Liturgical Press, 1980), 53.

4. Cardinal Roger Mahony, "Gather Faithfully Together," Supplement to *The Tidings* (Sept. 5, 1997): 4.

5. Eamonn Bredin, *Rediscovering Jesus: Challenge of Discipleship* (Quezon City, Philippines: Claretian Publications, 1986), 40.

6. Ben Witherington III, *The Jesus Quest: The Third Search for the Jew of Nazareth* (Downers Grove, IL: InterVarsity, 1995), 27.

DAY *4*

VOCATION AND DISCIPLESHIP

Luke 5:1–11

Peter is an attractive character in the Gospels. He is generous, enthusiastic, perhaps to a fault, with more confidence than self-knowledge, but there is something virile about him. We never have the sense that Peter is lazy. In Luke 5:1–11 we see him surrounded by his friends, fishermen, "cleaning up" after a day's work, washing his nets. He is minding his own business, not paying much attention to this lakeside preacher, but Jesus seeks him out, invites himself into his boat, tells him to put out for a catch. This encounter was to change his life, but he has no knowledge of that at the moment. He is still a fisherman, accommodating, a little skeptical: "Master, we have worked all night long but have caught nothing" (Luke 5:5). Still, he's ready to go along with this strange request. Peter the fisherman is about to become Peter the disciple.

Discipleship

Jesus did not come to found a church. He came to call men and women to discipleship for the sake of the kingdom of heaven. "Church" appears only three times in the Gospels, each time in Matthew. "Disciple" (*mathētēs*) appears more than 250 times in the New Testament, mostly in the Gospels and the Acts. The verb "to follow" (*akolouthē*) appears seventy times. Discipleship means following Jesus.

The concept of discipleship was not a new one; both the Pharisees and John the Baptist had disciples. But being a disciple of Jesus was unique in a number of ways. First, unlike the case of discipleship in Rabbinic Judaism, the disciples of Jesus did not choose the master; rather the master chose and called the disciples. The initiative always comes from Jesus (Mark 1:17; 2:14).

Second, there is an inclusive element to Jesus' call. He did not restrict it to the ritually pure and the religiously obedient; among those invited to follow him were "tax collectors and sinners." He was often criticized for associating with them (Mark 2:16). Women also accompanied him as disciples (Luke 8:2).

Third, Jesus' call to discipleship demands a radical change of heart (*metanoia*), a religious conversion often symbolized by leaving behind one's possessions. The story of the rich man in the Synoptic Gospels illustrates this theme. To this man who had kept all the commandments since his youth, Jesus said: "You lack one thing; go, sell what you own, and give the money to the poor, and you will have treasure in heaven; then come, follow me" (Mark 10:21). Thus discipleship means a clean break with one's past. Evangelical Christians speak of this as a "born again" experience. In the Gospels those who followed Jesus "left everything" (Luke 5:11). They left behind jobs (Mark 2:14), parents, family, and children (Luke 14:26). For some, discipleship also meant celibacy embraced for the sake of the kingdom (Matt 19:11–12). For others, married life and love gives form to their discipleship.

Fourth, being a disciple of Jesus means sharing in his ministry. Unlike the disciples of the rabbis who had to memorize their masters' teachings, the disciples of Jesus were called to minister as Jesus did. Jesus sent them out to teach and act in his name, to heal the sick, to cast out demons and free those troubled by evil spirits, and to proclaim that the reign of God was at hand (Mark 6:7–13; Luke 10:2–12). The disciples shared not just his ministry but his poverty and itinerant life as well (Matt 8:20). They would be members of his family, his brothers and sisters, those who hear the word of God and do it (Mark 3:34–35). Their attitude toward authority was to be respectful but not uncritical (Mark 12:17; Matt 23:2–3). He warned them that they would be rejected by others, persecuted by religious and civil authorities, even alienated from their own families (Matt 10:34–38).

Finally, being a disciple of Jesus means a willingness to love others with a love that is sacrificial and without conditions or limits. The disciples are to share whatever they have with others (Luke 6:30). They are to seek the last place and serve others (Mark 9:35). Nowhere is the ideal of discipleship as sacrificial love more clearly expressed than in John's Gospel, where Jesus says: "This is my commandment, that you love one another as I have loved you. No one has greater love than this, to lay down one's life for one's friends" (John 15:12–13).

The Call of the King

In the *Spiritual Exercises* St. Ignatius uses the image of Christ the King, calling others to join him in his mission, to express the idea of discipleship. Just before the second week begins, he invites the retreatant to contemplate the call of an earthly king, calling on those of generous spirits to join him in his campaign, pointing out the hardships they must be willing to endure: "those who would like to come with me must be content to eat as I eat, to drink and dress as I do and to labor like me in during the day and watch me throughout the night, so that having labored with me, they may have share with me in the victory" (no. 93). Here all Ignatius's romanticism comes to expression, his proud Hidalgo spirit fired with the vision of doing great things at great cost for a leader to whom one could give one's heart and soul.

Then he asks the retreatant to imagine this call coming from Christ our Lord, the eternal King. At the end of the contemplation, his love for Jesus leads him to pray, "Lord of all things, I make my offering with your help, in presence of your infinite Goodness and your glorious Mother and of all the Saints. I want and desire, if it be for your greater service and praise, to imitate you in bearing all injuries and all abuse and all poverty of spirit, even actual poverty, if you should choose to call me to such life" (no. 98).

Discipleship after Easter

After Easter the disciples came to understand that discipleship included following Jesus in his Easter passage from death to life. In his "way" section (8:27—10:52), Mark provides an extended instruction on discipleship. The way of Jesus means taking up one's cross and coming after him, taking the last place, even being willing to give up one's life (Mark 8:34–35). Thus Mark joins the idea of following Jesus with martyrdom, a notion very popular in the early Church which saw martyrdom as the highest expression of discipleship. Acts uses the word *disciple* to identify the early Christians, though this usage did not long endure. But the idea of discipleship, expressed in different ways, was important in the early Church.

The Cost of Discipleship

Discipleship thus means a personal and often costly following of Jesus that affects every dimension of human life. Like Ignatius's contemplation on the call of the king, it shapes a person's attitude toward property and wealth; affects one's human and erotic relationships; gives a new meaning to love; changes the way one understands success and personal fulfillment; and finally, calls one to enter deeply into Jesus' paschal mystery, his passage through death to life. At its heart is what the Christian tradition came to call the *Imitatio Christi,* the imitation of Christ.

Each of us has been called to live out the Christian call to discipleship in a particular way, whether as priest or deacon, religious or lay minister. For each of us, this is a very special vocation, one that has brought us great joy, but also one that has cost us a great deal.

It is often difficult to talk about the priesthood today. Many of us know of priests who are deeply unhappy, and we are very aware of the terrible cost of the failures of other priests. We forget that we have also known the joy of priesthood.

For many religious, their religious lives and communities have been diminished in the years following the Council. Some live an independence that scarcely distinguishes them from lay people. They long for a genuine experience of community and for communal prayer. Many have accepted the diminishment of their communities with a gracious spirit; they continue serving God generously in the vocations to which they know God has called them.

Deacons and lay ministers also can face discouragement. They want genuinely to serve, but their gifts are not always welcomed and esteemed. Many of those who have families have made great financial sacrifices for the sake of their ministry. They don't always have supportive communities, as many religious do. Some have experienced callous dismissals from their positions at the hands of less collegial pastors, without consideration for their personal situations.

Thus all of us have felt what Dietrich Bonhoeffer calls "the cost of discipleship."[1] And there is the wearing of the routine and the familiar that dulls the idealism that first drew us to ministry or religious life or priesthood, that sense of being called that once inspired so much generosity in us. When we look honestly at ourselves, no matter what our vocation, we often feel the need for personal renewal.

But not even our sinfulness can take away from God's call. In Luke, the story of the call of Peter takes on the character of a theophany. At the miraculous catch of fish Peter realizes that he is in the presence of the holy, and he is filled with a sense of his own unworthiness and sinfulness. He is afraid. He falls on his knees and says, "Go away from me, Lord, for I am a sinful man!" (Luke 5:8).

Like Peter, we have been made painfully aware of our own sinfulness; but it doesn't matter. Jesus saw the goodness, indeed the greatness in Peter. The God who knows us better than we can ever know ourselves sees so much more than our self-preoccupation and our sins. God knows our failings and our struggles. God reads the secrets of our hearts, sees the great desires as well as the disappointments, the strength as well as the weakness.

So often God seeks us out, discloses the holiness of his presence in our quiet moments and sometimes in our ministry. There are moments for each of us when our own lives become transparent to the presence of God working in and through us. At such times we become aware of the Spirit within our ministry: touching others, extending a reconciling hand to a person alienated from God or from the Church, accompanying someone who is in pain, or simply being present to someone in need. Sometimes when we are preaching, the Spirit unlocks something deep within us and we put aside our homily notes and find ourselves speaking directly from the heart. Or a word to another, spoken with concern, unlocks something deep within them, and heart speaks to heart. These are little epiphanies, special moments when the Spirit's presence in our lives becomes transparent. Afterwards we feel a deep sense of peace.

The last thing Peter expected was that this mysterious stranger would call him to be in his company. But his life was changed, as has been each of ours, by Jesus' call. Like the Twelve, we have been called to be with him, to be his companions (Mark 3:13–14).

Reflection Questions

1. How did I come to experience my vocation?

2. What does discipleship mean for me?

3. Where do I experience the cost of discipleship?

NOLI ME TANGERE: JESUS AND WOMEN

John 20:17

The Gospels mention a number of women who were particularly close to Jesus. The details are not always clear and later tradition has sometimes conflated their stories, but certainly some of these women were among Jesus' closest friends.

One of the closest was Mary of Magdala, known as Mary Magdalene. Her figure appears in all four Gospels. Given the fact that the Gospels reflect a male-centered culture that tended to suppress the stories of women, the many allusions to her suggest that she must have played a very important role in the history that lies behind the texts.

According to one New Testament tradition, present in both Matthew and John, Mary Magdalene was the first to whom the risen Jesus appeared. In Matthew, Jesus appears to Mary and the women who accompanied her to the tomb, telling them to bring the news to his brothers (Matt 28:9–10). In John, Jesus appears just to Mary with the same message, calling her by name. In this story as well, Jesus sends Mary to bring the good news of his resurrection to his brothers, the apostles. Because seeing the risen Lord and being sent on a mission constitutes the definition of an apostle for Paul, the Church as early as the third century gave Mary Magdalene the title *"apostolos apostolorum,"* apostle of the apostles, even though she is never explicitly called "apostle" in the Gospels.

Mary Magdalene also played an important role in the later tradition of the Church. An image of a woman on the wall of a third-century house church known as Dura-Europas in Syria is thought to represent her. She also appears in the apocryphal gospels of Thomas and Philip as well as the Gospel of Mary, though these Gnostic works did not become part of the biblical canon.

The image of Mary Magdalene was often conflated with the image of Mary of Bethany and that of the unnamed woman who washed the feet of Jesus with her tears (Luke 7:36–50); Pope Gregory the Great (d. 604) did this, mistakenly declaring that these three women were in fact the same. Others identified Mary Magdalene with the woman of Samaria (John 4:4–45) and the adulterous woman (John 8:1–11). Thus Mary, the disciple, friend of Jesus, and witness to the resurrection, became "the Magdalene," the penitent woman or reformed prostitute so much venerated in medieval piety and art.[2]

If there is no biblical or textual evidence for this story, it has remained very popular, especially in France where a cult of Mary Magdalene developed from the eighth century. Relics were supposedly found at Vézelay in 1265. Such relics were of course very important, able to turn a simple church into an important shrine for pilgrims with their financial offerings. Later hagiographers invented the story of Mary Magdalene's flight from Judaea, sojourn in Ephesus, and death at Aix en Provence. St. Maximin's, near Aix, also claimed to find her relics there in the thirteenth century (1279); although Vézelay tried to argue a "holy theft" of her relics, St. Maximin's cult gradually won out over that at Vézelay.

The Real Mary?

Who then was Mary Magdalene? The New Testament does not give us many details. Luke tells us simply that she was among the women who accompanied Jesus and ministered to him, and that he had driven seven demons out of her (Luke 8:1–3; cf. Mark 15:40–41). All four Gospels put her at the crucifixion. On Sunday morning she went to the tomb early to anoint the body of Jesus in the Synoptic tradition, and she was the first to whom Jesus appears, according to Matthew and John.

We can be confident that Mary of Magdala was a woman whose life had been transformed after her encounter with Jesus. She was apparently a troubled woman who had experienced a dramatic healing at his hands and remained henceforth in his company. Clearly she was a disciple. The Gospels give us a number of stories of men and women who had such a personal encounter with Jesus, went through a profound conversion that was both healing and liberating, and later played important roles among the disciples; among them are Peter (Luke 5:1–11; John 21:15–17), Paul (Phil 3:2–14), the Samaritan woman (John 4:4–41), and perhaps Zacchaeus (Luke 19:1–10).

The figure of Mary Magdalene in the Gospels has inspired a host of stories about her relationship with Jesus, from the more romantic versions in the Nikos Kazantzakis's novel *The Last Temptation of Christ* or Andrew Lloyd Weber's musical *Jesus Christ Superstar* to the obviously fanciful such as Dan Brown's *The Da Vinci Code*. The fascination with the relationship between Jesus and Mary Magdalene is understandable and not without some basis in fact. The Church has always taught the full humanity of Jesus, which means that all his relationships were deeply human ones; it takes nothing away from Jesus to suggest that he might have had romantic feelings toward one or other of the women he knew. In his lovely unfinished play, *Cristo: Una Tragedia Religiosa*, Federico García Lorca creates a fictional character, Esther, a childhood friend of Jesus who is deeply in love with him. As Jesus struggles to see his own path clearly, he knows he has to decide between a normal family life with her, with fields and flocks and children, or the life he feels called to by all "the stars that pierce [him] like knives."[3]

Mary of Magdala comes across in the Gospels as a woman who loved Jesus deeply and no doubt was loved deeply by him in return. Certainly their friendship was very close. We can take it for granted that Jesus would have had to appropriate his own sexuality, just as each of us must, that he may even have considered marriage. Beyond that there is simply no evidence that Jesus was anything but celibate. We should recognize Mary as a prominent disciple and leader in the early Christian movement whose influence has left an unmistakable imprint on the gospel tradition.

Other Women

Mary Magdalene was not the only woman in the Gospels who had a special relationship with Jesus. The sisters Martha and Mary of Bethany were also among them (John 11:1–44; cf. Luke 10:38–42). Andrew Greeley suggests that these two sisters were teenagers, "obviously very young because they were not yet married."[4]

Mark tells a story of a woman at Bethany anointing the head of Jesus with precious perfume (Mark 14:3–9); John tells a similar story, identifying the woman as Mary of Bethany, saying that she anointed the feet of Jesus and adding that she dried his feet with her hair, perhaps a detail borrowed from a similar story in Luke. But the story in its various forms is worth some reflection. For the woman to dry Jesus' feet with her hair suggests a gesture of particular intimacy, as in the culture of the time a woman would not unbind her hair in the presence of anyone but her husband. In the Markan story, Jesus rebukes those who criticize this apparent waste of the expensive ointment, saying that she has perfumed his body in preparation for his burial (Mark 14:8). This suggests that the woman knew something, perhaps from Jesus himself, that the other disciples had not yet realized.

Several other stories are worth mentioning. The woman at the well in Samaria (John 4:4–42) is transformed by her meeting with Jesus. The five husbands Jesus mentions may suggest, given the patriarchal culture in which a woman could not divorce her husband, that the woman had been victimized or abused by men. Regardless, through her encounter with Jesus, she becomes an evangelist, the one who brings her villagers to faith (John 4:42).

A final figure is that of the Syro-Phoenician woman which may reflect a historical incident. On meeting her, Jesus rather harshly spurns her request to heal her daughter, saying "it is not fair to take the children's food and throw it to the dogs" (Mark 7:27). Behind this probably lies the conviction that Jesus addressed himself only to the Jews, not to the Gentiles. But in her persistence, it is Jesus who is changed by the encounter, as he accedes to her request and heals her daughter.

Thus Jesus related easily and openly to women; they appear frequently in the gospel accounts and several are recognizable as among his close friends. The figure of Mary Magdalene continues to fascinate us. It is not too much to say that among his intimate friends were some women, because intimacy does not necessarily involve sexual expression. It means rather a relationship characterized by trust, mutual respect, even love, in which people are free to disclose their inner lives, their struggles, their fears, their fondest dreams and hopes. Such is the kind of relationship that Jesus desires with each of us.

Reflection Questions

1. Who are the people I can share my inner life with?

2. Do I take time to spend with them?

3. Do I have close friends of the opposite sex?

LEADERSHIP IN A CHANGING CHURCH

1 Corinthians 12

One of the great achievements of the Second Vatican Council was to develop a theology of the laity, stressing that through the sacraments of baptism and confirmation, lay men and women share in the mission of the Church, "appointed to this apostolate by the Lord himself" (*Lumen Gentium* 33). No longer was the "lay apostolate" described as "the collaboration of the laity in the apostolic tasks proper to the hierarchy"[5] as it had been in the decades before the Council, language which suggested that the mission or apostolate of the Church really belonged to the hierarchy. The laity also share in their own way in Christ's priestly, prophetic, and kingly functions; their vocation is to "seek the kingdom of God by engaging in temporal affairs" (*LG* 31). The lay apostolate is a participation in the mission of the Church itself: lay men and women are commissioned to that apostolate by the Lord sacramentally, through baptism and confirmation (*LG* 33).

The Council also began using ministry language, though somewhat hesitantly, in regard to the laity, opening up what would become in the postconciliar period the explosion of lay ministries in the Church. In this way the Council took a number of steps to recover the dignity of the vocation of the baptized. Postconciliar reflection would speak of baptism as the fundamental sacrament of ministry, whereas the role of the ordained priesthood is increasingly seen as a way to enable the priesthood of the baptized.

Thus a vocation to ministry involves not just discipleship but leadership. It includes "providing some sacred functions to the best of their ability" when ordained ministers are lacking (*LG* 35) and "expressing their opinion on matters for the good of the church" (*LG* 36). Pastorally, lay ministers share in Jesus' mission of calling others to discipleship, to form them, and to teach them how to be disciples (what evangelical Protestants speak of as "discipling"). The Christian community is in its essence a community of disciples. But as ministers we have an important leadership role to play.

An important dimension of ministerial leadership is the ability to sustain a vision of a renewed Church in a difficult time of transition and change such as our own. Brian Hehir, in a talk to the California Province of the Society of Jesus, referred to something John Courtney Murray said shortly after the end of Vatican II. Murray observed that the council had set afoot in the Church a process described as renewal and reform, and he proceeded to analyze the complexity of these two terms. Renewal, he said, is an affair of the intellect. It has about it the atmosphere of the library. Renewal is when you set out the vision of where you plan to go, designing the plan in grand strokes and broad themes. It is essentially visionary.

Reform, however, is an affair of institutions, changing them to serve the larger vision you have sketched. Reform has about it all the conflicted nature of the political arena.

He predicted that the challenge that the postconciliar Church would face would be that its vision of renewal would run ahead of its capability for reform. He said that those in positions of leadership would not be able to change institutions quickly enough to satisfy the visions the Council had let loose in the Church.

This is where Father Hehir made his point. He argued that the gap between renewal and reform is the gap that must be filled by leadership. He said that "leadership is the only way you can mediate between a living vision that is large and grand, and institutions that are not yet ready to support the vision. Leadership at every level: intellectual, administrative, pastoral, personal witness." In words that might describe the contemporary vocation of bishops, priests, and deacons, religious and lay ministers, he spoke of being signs of hope in the ecclesial community so that we live "in such a way that we continue to sustain the hope of the vision, and not let people be broken and fractured by institutions that are not yet ready to live the vision."[6]

How do we as ministers exercise this kind of leadership, filling the gap between the vision and a sometimes immobile Church? Can we mediate between the renewal begun by the Council and the reform that is not yet complete? This is never easy to do; it is often costly. Perhaps this was what Paul meant when he said: "in my flesh I am completing what is lacking in Christ's afflictions for the sake of his body, that is, the church" (Col 1:24).

Reflection Questions

1. What is my style of leadership?

2. What personal sacrifices do I join to the sacrifice of Christ?

Notes: Day Four

1. Dietrich Bonhoeffer, *The Cost of Discipleship* (New York: Macmillan, 1959).

2. See Susan Haskins, *Mary Magdalen: Myth and Metaphor* (New York: Riverhead Books, Harper Collins, 1995).

3. I am grateful to my colleague Cecilia González-Andrieu for bringing Lorca's work to my attention.

4. Andrew Greeley, *The Catholic Imagination* (Berkeley: University of California Press, 2000), 73.

5. Pius XII, "Allocution to Italian Catholic Action," *Acta apostolica sedis* 32 (1940): 362.

6. Father J. Bryan Hehir, "The Church in the United States: Jesuit Presence and Possibilities," a talk on the occasion of the California Province Assembly, Loyola Marymount University, August 8, 1996, 13–14 (unpublished).

DAY 5

TO MINISTER AS JESUS DID

Luke 22:24–27

In the midst of Luke's account of the Last Supper, just after the institution of the Eucharist, a dispute breaks out among the disciples over who among them is the greatest. Jesus responds:

> The kings of the Gentiles lord it over them; and those in authority over them are called benefactors. But not so with you; rather the greatest among you must become like the youngest, and the leader like the one who serves. For who is greater, the one who is at table or the one who serves? Is it not the one at table? But I am among you as one who serves. (Luke 22:25–27)

The passage occurs in each of the Synoptic Gospels, as well as in a variant form in 1 Peter 5:3 where the presbyters are instructed not to "lord it over" those assigned to them. It is often referred to by scholars as the "rank-dispute," for its *Sitz im leben,* its original context, is to be found in arguments over authority and leadership in the primitive Christian communities, disputes answered by appealing to Jesus' own understanding of himself as a servant (Mark 10:45; cf. John 13:13–15).

The fact that the early Christians adapted the Greek word *diakonos*, servant, to refer to those who exercised roles of leadership and authority in the community is based on Jesus' understanding of his death as an integral part of his own role as a servant, proclaiming and embodying God's reign, enacting it in gathering the lost and the alienated, healing the sick and those troubled by spirits of unfreedom, proclaiming the forgiveness of sin.

The office of the deacon as a specific ministry of compassionate service emerged by the end of the New Testament period. As assistants to the bishop, the deacons managed the temporal concerns of the Church and supervised its charitable works, serving as agents of the Church, dispensing gifts to the needy, and assisting in the ritual of baptism. Women also served as deacons in Western churches until the sixth century and as late as the twelfth century in the Eastern churches, though the order never completely disappeared.[1]

What does it mean to minister as Jesus did? Our understanding of ministry has changed considerably since the Second Vatican Council. The Council restored the permanent diaconate while the explosion of new ministries in the post-Vatican II Church has changed considerably the role of both priests and lay people in the Catholic community. Still Jesus should remain the model for all ministers.

Prior to the Council the priest occupied a privileged place within the Catholic culture. The sacral understanding of the priesthood that emerged from the Middle Ages defined priesthood almost exclusively in terms of the priest's role in the celebration of the Eucharist. Popularly, the priest was seen as a sacred person, equipped with sacramental powers so that he might offer the holy sacrifice of the Mass and "confect" the Eucharist. A priest was "another Christ," his role clearly defined and protected by a clerical culture. He was a man apart, separated from the laity by clerical dress and privilege, titles of respect, a single-sex educational system, rectory living, even the Latin language used in the liturgy. All this led to a primarily cultic understanding of priesthood.

The cultic model is still popular with some priests, and indeed has seen a kind of revival today. The report, "Charism of the Priesthood," done by the Oblate Renewal Center in San Antonio, Texas, observes that two models of priesthood are currently running on parallel ecclesial tracks: a servant-leader model that sees the priest finding his identity in preaching, presiding, serving, and empowering others within a community of ecclesial ministers, and a new or renewed cultic model that sees the priest as a sacred person, a man set apart to sanctify and mediate grace.[2]

Although there is some truth in each model, in my opinion they are not equally valid or helpful today. The demise of the sacral model of priesthood and the substitution of the word "presider" for "priest" in reference to eucharistic leadership has contributed to a loss of identity for many priests. The new emphasis on the cultic model by some priests and seminarians today reflects this loss of sacerdotal identity; it may represent a need to find security in status rather than service. But it is flawed theologically and does not realistically address our present reality.

Ministry with and for Others

The servant-leader model seems more in harmony with the changing ministerial demographics as well as the cultural changes that have so transformed the Catholic community in the United States. It suggests how sacerdotal ministry is to be exercised, if it is to meet the needs of tomorrow's Church. We all know how crucial leadership is, whether in a parish, a diocese, or at the level of the world Church. A leader who is open to others, able to dialogue, to listen and work with them, even to change, can make all the difference between a vital community and one that is moribund. But it is not just priests who are called to be servant-leaders.

Two characteristics essential to this kind of servant-leadership are colleagueship and collaboration. A minister can take a leadership role within a community only if he or she is a part of it, joined to its members by relationships of friendship and personal respect. This is especially true for priests. The time when the priest was the most educated member of the American Catholic community is long gone. Many parishioners today are college graduates, often with postgraduate degrees. Thus to be effective leaders today, priests must be able to work collaboratively with others: with deacons and professionally trained lay ministers, with religious women, with the well-educated men and women who sit on parish councils and boards, and with those from different ethnic communities.

It is rare today to hear the story of a person no longer active in the church because of a bad experience with a priest in confession. Not enough people go to confession today. But who has not heard the stories of those no longer active in the church because of unhappy experiences with a priest, deacon, or lay minister? I know of many young female graduates from our university who went on to take graduate degrees in theology or pastoral ministry, anxious to work for the church. But not all of them were able to find a comfortable place to do so. A good number of them gave it their best effort, but ultimately left church ministry because of the inability of the priests they encountered to share responsibility with lay professionals, to work as colleagues with them. Such cases represent a terrible waste of talent and dedication, not to say of injury and hurt of good people.

Many deacons and lay ministers are looking for priests who can enable them in their own ministries and share with them responsibility for the life and direction of the community. They are willing to help, but only if their own competence is acknowledged. Thus, a crucial part of pastor's role is to be able to discern the gifts or charisms present in the community and to enable those so gifted to use them. We all know of cases where a pastor who models a collaborative approach to ministry is succeeded by one who immediately dismisses the parish board, ignores or replaces its pastoral team, and tries to make all the decisions by himself. For the vitality of the parish, the result is disaster.

All ministers, ordained or lay, must be able to share their authority, to listen to an honest difference of opinion, even to criticism. They must be able to relate to all the different groups within the community, and to help them learn from one another. They must be able to welcome the competence of others, to seek and build consensus. To be leaders they must also know how to be colleagues as well.

Reflection Questions

1. In what ways is my ministry an example of servant leadership?

2. Whose ministry have I enabled?

3. Who enables my ministry?

IN EARTHEN VESSELS
2 Corinthians 3–5

The dispute over rank is not the only example of conflicts over authority and ministry in the early Church. Unfortunately there are others. Paul's authority as an apostle was challenged by those he sarcastically calls "super apostles" in the church at Corinth (2 Cor 10–12). Some may have been sophisticated, polished speakers, whose very grace and style made Paul seem inferior by comparison (cf. 2 Cor 11:5–6). Some went so far as to ridicule both his personality and his preaching: "His letters are weighty and strong, but his bodily presence is weak, and his speech contemptible" (2 Cor 10:10). Paul must have been deeply hurt by the personal nature of their criticism.

In response, he develops what is perhaps one of the most beautiful descriptions of the Church's apostolic ministry we find in the New Testament. He writes that he doesn't have to justify himself; his confidence comes not from his own accomplishments but from God in Christ "who has made us competent to be ministers of a new covenant" (2 Cor 3:6), bearers of a ministry written not on tablets of stone but on the flesh of their hearts. It is a ministry in the Spirit of Jesus, bringing freedom, enabling them to gaze on the Lord's glory with unveiled faces, transforming them into the very image of the Lord.

Paul then will not give in to discouragement. Indeed, there is an iconic quality to the apostolic ministry that he exercises. He tells the Corinthians, "we do not proclaim ourselves; we proclaim Jesus Christ as Lord and ourselves as your slaves for Jesus' sake"

(2 Cor 4:5). In preaching always Christ, he is confident that God who has shown in the hearts of his ministers will make known the glory of God shining on the face of Christ (2 Cor 4:6). In spite of afflictions, doubts, even persecutions, they carry in their bodies the dying of Jesus, so that the life of Jesus might be revealed, revealed in their flesh (2 Cor 4:11).

Still, convinced as he is of his call and ministry in the power of the Spirit, Paul is well aware that we possess this treasure in earthen vessels, "so that it may be made clear that this extraordinary power belongs to God and does not come from us" (2 Cor 4:7). There is a fragile quality to his ministry, one of which we ourselves are so well aware; the vessel can be broken, its power lost.

Thus, even in the face of jealousy, criticism, and personal attack, Paul proclaims his ministry as a ministry of reconciliation, received from God who has reconciled us to himself through Christ. "So we are ambassadors for Christ, since God is making his appeal through us," calling the Corinthians to be reconciled to God (2 Cor 5:20).

In spite of his efforts and the power of his appeal, the church at Corinth was still troubled by jealousy and quarreling over its ministry fifty years later, as we know from another letter to the Corinthian church, written at the end of the first century by a leader of the church of Rome known to us as Clement. Certain members of the community, apparently jealous of the authority of the presbyters, had ejected them from their office. To address this, Clement begins with a long and sad history of jealousy in the story of God's people that begins with Cain and his brother Abel and reaches all the way to the "greatest and most righteous pillars of the Church" in his time, Peter and Paul. He even suggests that the jealousy of others was responsible for Peter's death (1 Clement 5:4).[3]

Thus disputes over authority are nothing new in the history of the Church. The exercise of authority always puts its bearers at risk. The power that comes with authority is open to abuse, and we carry the grace of our ministry in fragile earthen vessels. We must live so as to be worthy of the gift. And even the faithful exercise of ministry can occasion jealous and envy in others.

Facing Criticism

Thus those who take on ministerial roles in the Church should expect criticism. Jesus himself continually faced it in his ministry. His own family thought he was out of his mind (Mark 3:21). He was called a glutton and drunkard, a friend of tax collectors and sinners for his inclusive practice of table fellowship (Matt 11:19; cf. Mark 2:16). He was criticized because his disciples didn't fast like those of the Pharisees (Mark 2:18), accused of violating the Sabbath for his acts of compassion (Mark 3:2; Luke 6:2, 7; John 9:16), and charged with being in league with the devil for his exorcisms (Luke 1:15), even of being possessed himself (John 8:48).

It's of course never easy to accept criticism, especially from those close to us. We tend to take it personally, which might indicate that we have become overly identified with a particular role or office. Or we see it as a betrayal of friendship, although it might just be evidence of concern on the part of someone who really does care for us.

Unfair criticism is always the most difficult to accept and live with. An instinctive reaction is to lash back or try to get even. If we can distance ourselves from our personal feelings, we might learn something about how others see us, or how we might carry out our responsibilities more effectively. Sometimes we can do no more than to try to bear criticism, especially unfair criticism with that same kind of openness to the other that Jesus showed in his passion.

Nothing has illustrated more clearly the fragile character of the Church's office of ministry than the recent revelations of the sexual abuse by priests. The scandal has shocked the faithful, ruined the lives of so many young people, robbing them of their faith, and done great damage to the morale of priests. These are sins of the institution, not of all priests. Those priests who have struggled to live their chastity with integrity have had others look at them suspiciously simply because they are priests; it has been a terrible burden and tarnished the reputation of a vocation that they love.

Some priests, falsely accused, have experienced their own Calvary. I know one, an older pastor who should have been enjoying his retirement but stayed on because of the shortage of priests. He was accused by a man whose story changed so often that it was deemed incredible by the former FBI agent assigned to investigate the charges for the archdiocese. The charges were dismissed and the priest remained in his ministry, but he had to endure the humiliation of having a letter, which reviewed the case and detailed the charges, read in his presence at all the Masses one Sunday in his parish.

We possess this treasure in earthen vessels.

Reflection Questions

1. Where have I suffered from the criticism of others?

2. How has my own critical attitude hurt others?

3. What might compromise the integrity of my ministry?

PREACHING AND PRESIDING

Luke 4:14–32

One of the things that Pope John Paul II will be most remembered for, along with the great role he played in the collapse of the iron curtain, will be his emphasis on evangelization, or what he often refers to as the "new evangelization." This is the real work of the Church, not self-maintenance, but proclaiming the Gospel to others, to those who have not yet heard the message and to the millions who have forgotten it, the good news of what God has done in Jesus. This concern for evangelization must be at the heart of Christian ministry; it should inspire our preaching and be evident in our presiding.

How often have we heard that what makes the difference between a vital and successful parish and one that is lifeless is the quality of its liturgy? For priests especially, good preaching and presiding are particularly important, given their role of presiding at the Eucharist. But an increasing number of deacons and lay ministers are called on to preach and preside today at noneucharistic services: at prayer and Bible services; at ecumenical gatherings; at baptisms, weddings, and funerals in the case of deacons; and particularly for those parish life directors who are responsible for guiding communities in the absence of a priest, leading them when they gather for prayer and communion services.

Preaching

Many today are hungry for the Word. But how do we proclaim the Gospel in the face of today's widespread secularization and religious indifference; how do we witness to its social dimensions in the face of the crushing poverty that affects so many; how can we help others come to that "personal and profound meeting with the Savior" called for by Pope John Paul II in his 1990 encyclical, *Redemptoris Missio* (no. 44); how can we share our personal faith experience with others struggling to clarify their own? Unfortunately many today, especially Hispanic Catholics, seem to be finding their meeting with Jesus through the preaching of Evangelical and Pentecostal Christians.

Evangelical preaching means being able to articulate the religious experience of a community of faith and to call each to be a disciple, not just a member. It means empowering others by helping them discover the power of the Word. It means finding ways to address the many who are inactive or unchurched.

After years of teaching, I continue to be amazed at how unfamiliar my students are with scripture, and how little they understand what the biblical text is really saying. So when I'm teaching scripture, I spend a good deal of time in class not lecturing, but having them read a passage and then unpack it. What is going on in this text? To what do these images refer? How does the language and imagery pick up and expand on a theme seen much earlier in the book or in the Bible as a whole? Does it foreshadow some fulfillment yet to come?

I also find this approach very helpful in preaching. Often I preach with the missalette in hand, standing at the head of the aisle rather than at the lectern so that I can better see how people are reacting, working through the three readings, unpacking the imagery, making the connections with the other readings and with their lives. Often the scriptures come alive, first for me, then for the congregation.

Perhaps the most difficult part of preparing a homily is not finding a creative way to develop some particular theme, but first, finding the good news contained in the text, and then working out the connection between the good news and the experience of the members of the community. What is on their minds? Where are they struggling? How do the readings address those concerns? A good homily is one that is able to articulate their struggles and concerns and illumine them in the light of the Word.

An effective preacher is one who can embrace those concerns and reflect on them with them with the congregation rather than preaching at them. Nothing is more off-putting than the preacher who talks down to a congregation, who says habitually "you," rather than "we." As Robert Schwartz has written, in the effective homilist, "Leadership and membership must come together."[4]

Presiding

How do we become successful presiders? For me, good presiding involves first, a combination of reverence and hospitality, and second, the ability to share the celebration with others. A good presider must have a sense for the mysterious divine presence as well as a consciousness of the diverse nature of the liturgical assembly.

First, reverence. I think we've come a long way from the "groovy" liturgies of the 70s and early 80s, but it still takes considerable skill and sensitivity to combine a nonstuffy, hospitable atmosphere with a reverence appropriate to the mystery we celebrate.

Taizé, the ecumenical monastic community high on a ridge in Burgundy, France is always a good model. The prayer at Taizé is wonderful for its unabashed but restrained piety. It communicates a reverence that is contagious, a spirit of prayer and sense of the sacred that is evident everywhere, from the atmosphere of the dark church illuminated by the candles before the icons, the music that carries the prayer, the young people who meet you at the doors of the Church of the Reconciliation with signs proclaiming "silence" in different languages, to the worshippers kneeling or prostrating in prayer on the floor. Taizé is rich in color, symbol, silence, and song. One experiences sacred space at Taizé, unlike the "beige" churches described by Robert Barron, "structures that are largely void of symbolism, imagery iconography, and narrativity."[5]

Second, good presiding means finding ways to give expression to the true nature of the community gathered for prayer as a liturgical assembly. If we look at the liturgical vocabulary of the first millennium, it is clear that all celebrate and that all offer the sacrifice. The *General Instruction* which introduces the *Roman Missal Revised by Decree of the Second Vatican Council* (1970) regards the entire assembly as the primary agent of the liturgical action.[6] Our liturgical assemblies should reflect this fact. But to do so requires something of a change of consciousness on the part of those who preside.

Some priests still operate out of the "my Mass" mentality; their liturgical style tends to center the liturgy around themselves, reducing others to passive spectators. This does not properly image a community at worship. An assembly-centered liturgy seeks to share responsibility for the liturgical celebration with all present, under the leadership of the presider. Some priests might improve their presidential style simply by observing some of their brother priests.

Reflection Questions

1. Is there an evangelical dimension to my ministry?

2. How do I seek out the inactive or the unchurched?

3. What is the focus of my presidential style: Is it me or the Lord?

DO NOT BE AFRAID

Mark 6:45–52

After the miracle of the loaves, Jesus dismisses his disciples and withdraws into the mountains to pray. In the middle of the night, as the disciples battle a stormy sea, he comes to them walking on the water. When he draws near to the disciples he says, "Take heart, it is I; do not be afraid" (Mark 6:50).

The story is obviously a theophany with Jesus walking on the water as Yahweh walks on the water in the Hebrew Scriptures. Mark adds this strange little verse, "he intended to pass them by," recalling for those listening the image of Yahweh passing by Moses in Exodus (Exod 33:22), or the passage in Job where he walks on the waters (Job 9:8–11). What Jesus tells the disciples in Mark is his message to us: he is close, even when we seem most alone; we have nothing to fear. One finds the same message in the Gospel of John. John says that perfect love casts out all fear (1 John 4:18).

Love Casts Out Fear

We all have areas in our lives where our love is not yet perfect, where our trust is less than it might be, and we are afraid. We worry about how we come across to others, about our inadequacies, about failing. We worry about getting old, about not being in control, about having to let go of some position or place. We fear sickness and ill-health. We fear death.

The late Cardinal Bernardin was a wonderful example of someone who faced the challenges in his life with an equanimity that bespoke a deep interior life. He showed remarkable courage, both in the face of his cancer and in the terrible trial of false accusation. Even in those moments, he was able to reach out to others, including to his accuser.

When he died, I read everything I could find about him. In one article in a Chicago paper I found a story about his first days as the city's new archbishop. Shortly after arriving he asked to join a group of priests that met regularly for prayer, and they welcomed him. But they also challenged him, about his lifestyle, his values, particularly about his relationship with Jesus. And he responded to those challenges, admitting later that he took a number of steps to rearrange his life, in particular, making regular prayer a part of it.

Judging from the grace with which he faced both the false charges and his final illness, he must have come to that interior knowledge of Jesus which Ignatius speaks of in the *Exercises*. May we also come to that deep personal knowledge and love of our Lord in these days of retreat.

Reflection Questions

1. Of what am I most afraid?

2. Who are some of the really courageous people in my life?

Notes: Day Five

1. Kyriaki Karidoyanes FitzGerald calls attention to a growing desire to restore the order of deaconesses in many of the eastern churches; "Women Deacons? An Eastern Orthodox Perspective," *Origins* 35/35 (2006): 587.

2. Lea Woll, lecture on "Emerging Patterns of Priestly Service," in *The Charism of the Priesthood,* March 1997 colloquium of the National Federation of Priests' Councils 8/2 (Chicago: NFPC, 1997), 5.

3. See J. B. Lightfoot, *The Apostolic Fathers* (Grand Rapids, MI: Baker House Books, 1987), 15.

4. Robert M. Schwartz, *Servant Leaders of the People of God* (Mahwah, NJ: Paulist Press, 1989), 142.

5. Robert Barron, *Bridging the Great Divide: Musings of a Post-Liberal, Post-Conservative Evangelical Catholic* (Lanham, MD: Rowman and Littlefield Publishers, 2004), 269.

6. Robert Cabié, *The Church at Prayer, Vol. II,* ed. Georges Martimort (Collegeville, MN: The Liturgical Press, 1986), 191–92.

DAY 6

THE *IMITATIO CHRISTI*

Philippians 3:10–11

Thomas à Kempis' little book, *The Imitation of Christ,* has been surpassed only by the Bible itself in terms of its devotional influence. The author was most probably a fifteenth-century member of the Brethren of the Common Life, a community of secular priests and laity founded in the Netherlands by Geert de Groote (1340–1384). The title is well chosen, for the imitation of Christ lies at the very heart of the Christian life. St Paul writes about how his own life since his conversion has been patterned on the life of Christ: "I want to know Christ and the power of his resurrection and the sharing of his sufferings by becoming like him in his death, if somehow I may attain the resurrection from the dead" (Phil 3:10–11).

Martyrdom

For many throughout Christian history, witnessing to Christ has indeed cost them their lives. Justin Martyr (c. 160), a philosopher turned Christian apologist describes how the courage showed by persecuted Christians led him to the faith: "When I was a disciple of Plato," he writes, "hearing the accusations made against the Christians and seeing them intrepid in the face of death and of all that men fear, I said to myself that it was impossible that they should be living in evil and in the love of pleasure" (II Apol. 18, 1).

Susan Bergman's book on contemporary martyrs points out that by various estimates, the twentieth century—the "tyrant century" in the words of Osip Mandelstam, martyred in Russia—has produced more Christian martyrs than any other, perhaps as many as 26 million.[1] Her book is a collection of moving portraits by contemporary writers of some of those men and women, among them Oscar Romero, Simone Weil, Janani Luwum, Nate Saint, Martin Luther King, and the Jesuit martyrs of El Salvador.

Each story is unique and moving. Simone Weil was a French activist and mystic, born of Jewish parents, who died at the age of thirty-four in a British sanatorium, probably the result of her insistence on eating no more than the official ration allowed to her compatriots in France during the Second World War, in spite of the fact that she had tuberculosis. Janani Luwum was the Anglican archbishop of Kampala who was tortured and killed by Idi Amin. Nate Saint was killed with his missionary companions in Ecuador in 1956 as they tried to make contact with the Huaorani Indians, a story recently dramatized in the movie, *End of the Spear.* Some have pushed forward the definition of martyrdom, for example, Maria Goretti, whose story is told in Kathleen Norris's wonderful essay "Maria Goretti—Cipher or Saint." Norris challenges the popular picture of the young Italian girl as a martyr for chastity; instead she sees her as one whose particular witness was a courageous resistance to evil, combined with the ability to forgive the man who took her life as she lay dying, an act of grace that contributed ultimately to the man's conversion. Others were martyred for their unwillingness to bend their faith to the demands of political authority or to admit evil into their lives.

What struck me particularly as I read Bergman's book was the recurring theme, that so many of these contemporary martyrs saw their own deaths as an offering or sacrifice, uniting them to the sacrifice of Christ. Charles de Foucauld, whose vision of the spirituality of Jesus' hidden life at Nazareth led him to a life of solidarity with the impoverished tribesmen of the Sahara; Edith Stein, the converted Jewish philosopher and later Carmelite nun, who said to her frightened sister Rosa as the Gestapo took them from her convent in Holland to transport them to Auschwitz, "Come, let us go for our people"; Etty Hillesum, another Jew drawn to Christianity, who rejoiced to be "at the center of all human suffering"; in her diary, her last words before she too vanished at Auschwitz were, "We should be willing to act as a balm for all wounds." Also included are the stories of Maximilian Kolbe, the Polish Conventual Franciscan who volunteered to take the place of another prisoner in the Auschwitz death cell, and Dietrich Bonhoeffer, whose often misunderstood phrase "this-worldliness of Christianity" meant for him living unreservedly life's duties as a watching with Christ in Gethsemane.

I recently visited the convent of St. Maria vom Frieden in the old city of Cologne which Edith Stein entered in 1933, in the same year Hitler came to power. She came from a nonreligious Jewish family from Breslau, now Wroclaw in Poland. A brilliant young woman, she studied at Göttingen and then Freiburg under Edmund Husserl, the founder of phenomenology, and became one of his most famous students. After reading the life of St. Teresa of Avila (who was also from a family with Jewish roots) she exclaimed, "This is the truth." She was baptized in 1922, and after finishing her doctorate taught for a number of years at a Dominican convent school, St. Magdalena, in Speyer.

In 1933 she entered Carmel where she continued her academic work, though now writing on the mystical life and translating some works such as John Henry Newman's The *Idea of a University*. After Kristallnacht (1938), the night of the broken glass on which the Nazis attacked synagogues and Jewish shops throughout Germany, she moved to the Carmelite convent in Echt, the Netherlands, as even her presence in Cologne endangered the sisters there. Here she wrote her great work, the *Science of the Cross*. In 1942, shortly after the Dutch bishops had spoken out publicly against the persecution of the Jews, the Nazis arrested all the Catholic Jews in Holland. Edith and her sister Rosa, staying in the convent at Echt, were picked up by the Gestapo on August 2, transported east, and died at Auschwitz on August 9. Edith Stein, Sister Teresia Benedicta a Cruce as she was known in the community, was canonized on October 11, 1998.

In the final essay of Bergman's book, one of the writers, a non-Catholic, quotes Pope John Paul II in a contemporary martyrology of his own composing, saying of this great multitude, "They have completed in their death as martyrs the redemptive suffering of Christ."

The book is powerful because it takes seriously the efforts of each martyr sketched to enter into his or her life fully. These were real men and women who faced honestly the challenges their lives brought them. Many could have escaped their fate, but chose not to. Their holiness lies not in avoiding the implications of their humanity, position, or vocation, but precisely in entering into it fully. It is the call of every Christian to face whatever difficult challenges life brings—its often damaged relationships, its difficult choices, its demand for facing problems and for thinking critically, its struggles, even its injustices—and to transform all through the power of the Gospel. I found particularly moving that so many saw their own suffering as a participation in the paschal mystery of Jesus. This used to be a dimension of our Christian life, which we learned as children, but which many today have lost sight of. It is a mystical vision of communion in Christ's sacrifice.

Reflection Questions

1. In what ways do I seek to practice the *Imitatio Christi*?

2. Which contemporary martyrs speak most powerfully to me?

AN EMBODIED SPIRITUALITY

1 John 1:1–8

While the Greek word *martyrein* itself means witness, not all witnessing is done at the cost of one's life. For most Christians, their fundamental witness comes not through their deaths, but by the ways they live out their lives.

Toward the end of the New Testament period, the communities reflected in the Johannine epistles found themselves locked in a struggle with certain members influenced by Gnosticism. Like most Gnostics, who disregarded the significance of embodied existence, teaching that salvation came through their spiritual knowledge, these Gnostic Christians were unconcerned about the way they lived their lives. They had been baptized and were spirit-filled people and that was enough. Gnosticism is always nervous about the body, about embodied existence. Some Gnostics preferred to ignore it, seeing sexual expression as defiling and seeking salvation through gnosis, a kind of intellectual spirituality. Others argued that sexual immorality is of no account, because they already were living in the spirit. The "Christ" party at Corinth may have reflected this tendency, arguing that they were beyond ordinary laws or conventional morality (cf. 1 Cor 8:12–20).

In replying to Gnostic tendencies in his communities, the author of 1 John emphasizes the bodily humanity of Jesus: he came in the flesh, he really shed his blood, and he—as we must—entered into the final mystery of death, and was raised up.

Hence he stresses that Jesus came "not with the water only but with the water and the blood" (1 John 5:6).

Contemporary Gnosticism

Gnostic spirituality is by no means a thing of the past; we have a number of modern versions. One of its most obvious contemporary expression attempts to privatize spirituality and divorce it from religion. Part of the fascination with Dan Brown's book, *The Da Vinci Code,* with its privileging of the Gnostic literature over the canonical texts of the early Church, the New Testament, is precisely its reduction of spirituality to something private and personal. One of the most significant differences between the Gnosticism and orthodox Christianity was that for the Gnostics, salvation was understood as personal enlightenment for a spiritual elite, a secret knowledge mediated by the Gnostic literature.

Thus in many ways historic Gnosticism is surprisingly contemporary. Like the ancient Gnostics, many today see the major spiritual problem not as sin, but as ignorance. Orthodox Christianity, on the other hand, has from the beginning proclaimed the story of the life, death, and resurrection of Jesus as a message that liberates us from sin and transforms us. It was not a secret knowledge for a spiritual elite, but essentially public and missionary, good news for all to hear. The Gnostic provenance of the Gospel of Thomas is evident from its opening line: "These are the secret words which the living Jesus spoke and Didymus Judas Thomas wrote down."

Elaine Pagels is a scholar who prefers Gnostic to orthodox Christianity. But she accurately observes that the orthodox Christians "were concerned—far more than Gnostics—with their relationships with other people."[2] If Gnosticism was a solitary faith, orthodox Christianity was essentially communal. Perhaps this is why Gnosticism is so popular today, particularly with those who like to say "I'm very spiritual, but not religious."

Another contemporary form of Gnosticism reduces the good news of our salvation in Christ Jesus to a kind of spiritual therapy. For many middle class Americans, Jesus' new life is seen as something that brings about self-actualization and healing from personal tragedies, psychological wounds, dysfunctional families, addictive behavior, codependency, workaholism, and other forms of inauthentic existence. Spirituality means getting one's life together, reducing stress, or avoiding burnout, but little is said about conversion of life, witnessing to the kingdom, and entering into the paschal mystery of Jesus now and at the hour of our death.

The basic metaphor is Jesus as healer and friend, the tolerant Jesus, the one who makes everything OK, not the Jesus of the Gospels who makes demands on us. Its ecclesiological tendency is to see the church as an ideal, healing community, and many move from one community or tradition to another until they find a comfortable fit. Think of the popularity of books about healing with spiritual overtones like those of Scott Peck, Thomas Moore, and Deepak Chopra.

Against this tendency to avoid the more unpleasant implications of our embodied existence, the author of 1 John reminds us of the reality of the incarnation: that Jesus came in the flesh, that he conquered the world through his union with the Father and sacrificial death. An embodied spirituality cannot afford to ignore issues of affectivity, health, relationship, and sexuality. We are not angels, disembodied intellects. We are our bodies, male and female, created in the image and likeness of God (Gen 1:27). Our bodies express our spirits; through them we relate to others and the world. Therefore we should care for our bodies, be careful of our health, get proper exercise (a kind of asceticism), and observe an appropriate modesty in our manner and dress. Our affectivity puts us in touch with our deepest desires, the basis for the discernment of spirits, so important for recognizing God's movement in our lives. We are sexual beings; to refuse to acknowledge our sexual nature, including our sexual orientation, is to deny a part of ourselves. Our fundamental posture becomes dishonest; denial hides at the heart of who we are. We are also social beings. As we have seen, Christianity, unlike Gnosticism, is concerned with relationships with other people. It is here that our faith becomes real; we cannot be disciples of Jesus all by ourselves.

As disciples of Jesus, we are called to take part in his paschal mystery, a theme constant in the New Testament; it appears in the Synoptics, in St. Paul, and in John. If some Christian spirituality in the past has made a cult out of suffering and pain, that should not cause us to write out the place of suffering in Christian life. It is unavoidable.

In the Gospels Jesus says that being a disciple means to deny yourselves, take up your cross, and come follow him. Our Christian life is to be an *Imitatio Christi,* including imitating him by entering into his paschal mystery.

Reflection Questions

1. Where do I experience most the embodied nature of my spirituality?

2. What three people have most influenced me by their example?

CELIBACY AND COMMUNITY

Luke 18:18–30

Celibacy is difficult for many people to understand. They wonder about how many priests and religious are faithful to their commitment to celibacy, or dismiss those who are as emotionally underdeveloped. In *The Priest,* a terribly biased movie, those priests who violated their vows were honest, warm, and genuine figures, while those who kept them were portrayed as desiccated, angry, alcoholic, and hypocritical—not much encouragement there. But we don't need movies like this to caricature celibate living. We've seen enough of the damage that can be done by those who fail to develop a healthy celibate life, and are only too aware of the damage this failure has done to the priesthood and religious life.

At an ordination, retired bishop Francis A. Quinn once spoke eloquently of the call to celibacy as a challenge in a time of sexual revolution and intense emphasis on genitality. "Celibacy," he told the *ordinandi,* "is not something we possess for once and for all. We are constantly becoming celibate. Because of our upbringing, because of possible unenlightened sexual repression in early years, because of the original clouding of intellect and the weakening of will, because of the need for intimacy, and because of the downright pleasure of genitality, you will find celibacy an unremitting challenge."[3]

But when celibacy is lived honestly and with integrity, it can be a great gift. Few people have written as movingly on celibate men and women as the monastic-friendly poet Kathleen Norris, author of *Cloister Walk*. She says a celibacy that works is one practiced by people who are fully aware of their sexuality, but are able to express it in a celibate way; it means accepting sublimation as a normal part of adulthood. The fruit of such a healthy celibacy is hospitality and a gift for friendship with all people, men and women, old and young.[4]

Most celibates sense the liabilities of a celibate life and struggle to live it honestly. If their chastity is lived with integrity, it uncovers within them a profound vulnerability, an emptiness that only God can fill. It can be the desert wherein they encounter the Lord.

There are of course many ways of coping with chastity that are less than honest. Celibate living should not lead to a rejection of close relationships. There are some who out of fear erect walls around themselves, shutting themselves off from genuine human contact as much as possible. There is no affectivity in their lives, except anger. Others try to fill the void with surrogate satisfactions, various kinds of dependencies—alcoholism, workaholism, careerism, compulsive shopping, possessions, power. Others pursue clandestine relationships, leading double lives.

It is particularly difficult to live a celibate life in a sensate and individualistic culture like our own. That individualism has affected many priests and religious. Many work and live as "Lone Rangers." Others ask their fellow priests or religious if they have any real commitment to each other or why they do not find more support from one another. Many people today argue that celibacy makes a great deal of sense for a religious priest whose vocation implies a commitment to community. But what about the diocesan priest? Is there no communal dimension to his vocation, no sense of solidarity with others who have a similar ecclesial mission?

A reflection on the development of the church's pastoral office shows that there has been a collegial or communal dimension to this ministry from the beginning. Though we tend to think of Paul an individualist, a careful reading of his letters reveals that he always worked with others, including women; he refers frequently to his "workers" *(ergatēs, kopiontēs)*, "co-workers" *(sunergoi),* and "brothers" *(adelphoi).* Similarly, the New Testament names for local church leaders appear always in the plural: "leaders" or "presiders" (1 Thes 5:12; Rom 12:8), "prophets and teachers" (1 Cor 12:28; Acts 13:1), "bishops and deacons" (Phil 1:1), "leaders" (Heb 13:7, 17, 24), "pastors and teachers" (Eph 4:11). The word *presbyter,* from which our English word *priest* is derived etymologically, almost always appears in the plural. This usage suggests a collegial character to the ministry of local church leadership from the beginning. Even the Latin term *ordinare* (to ordain) means "to order," in the sense of incorporating one within an order or group, of deacons, of presbyters, or of bishops.

If the Church's pastoral office was originally exercised collegially, we need to ask whether our own experience today is of a truly collegial ministry. Celibacy without community is very difficult to sustain emotionally. Do we find solidarity and mutual support in our priestly vocation, or is our experience one of finding celibacy a burden that cuts us off from community with others, particularly from those with whom we should have most in common? I remember one diocesan priest who lectured me at some length about how he, unlike religious, had chosen a life without community. Years later I found out that he had sexually abused several boys in his parish.

With fewer priests today and with the loss of so much of the clerical culture of the past, presbyteral solidarity will become even more important. Priests need some community beyond the parish to sustain them emotionally. Without a spouse to challenge and correct them, it is too easy to lapse into the immature self-centeredness and petulance with which we are all familiar. A good parish can provide considerable support and satisfaction for a dedicated priest, but our parishes are generally very family oriented. Priests need something more.

There are some possibilities. Priests from several neighboring parishes could join together for personal sharing and prayer or to share reflections on the readings for the coming Sunday's homily. In areas where the different Christian churches follow a common lectionary, this might be done ecumenically. Some priests gather regularly in support groups such as *Jesu caritas* which facilitate communication with colleagues and friends on a deeper level. There could be more experimentation with the team-ministry concept, where priests serving several adjacent communities might live together for companionship and mutual support. Or a base community could develop within a parish, consisting of its ordained and lay ministers, gathering regularly for prayer, perhaps centering on the Liturgy of the Hours.

Thus there is much that priests and other ministers who are celibate can do for each other. We all need friends to relax with, companions with whom we can share a pasta dinner or sushi lunch. We need friends with whom we can share our personal struggles, who will give us honest feedback, and rejoice with us in our successes. Which of us does not need close friends with whom we can share our inner selves, our hopes and fears, our confusion and frustration, the forbidden areas of our lives, our relationship with God?

Reflection Questions

1. Who is my spiritual confidant?

2. Who are the friends with whom I can share my inner life?

3. What community sustains me?

DISCERNING THE SPIRIT

1 John 4:1

Beloved, do not believe every spirit,
but test the spirits to see whether they are from God.[5]

Discernment is at the heart of the *Spiritual Exercises* of St. Ignatius, helping the retreatant to discover the direction in which God is leading him or her. Comparing it to panning for gold, Wilkie Au and Noreen Cannon Au describe discernment as "a way of sifting through the complex desires embedded in our hearts. The process involves retrieval, evaluation, and selection."[5]

Ignatius began to learn about discernment in observing his own affectivity early in his conversion. He tells the story in his autobiography. Bored during his long convalescence in his parents' home at Loyola after the injury he received at Pamplona, he asked for some books, hoping to read the courtly romances that had so fired his imagination earlier in his life. But there were no such books at Loyola; instead they gave him the book of the gospels and another on the lives of the saints, and for want of anything more to his liking, he began to read them.

But his reading began to have an effect on him. He noticed that when he returned to pursuing his romantic fantasies and dreams of knightly glory, he would be momentarily filled with enthusiasm, but afterwards, he would experience emptiness and dryness. But when he read the lives of the saints and began thinking about imitating them, he would feel himself drawn by the idea of doing great things for the Lord, and he would experience a peace that would last for hours. From his careful observation of his own affectivity and the notes he jotted down, he eventually was to develop what he called the rules for the discernment of spirits.

Discernment is essential for those in ministry today. So often they find themselves caught in the middle, between pastor and people, between the parish and the bishop, or between others in positions of authority. And there are different problems that any minister today must face: tensions in the Church, different groups and factions asking for support, difficult moral choices, issues of being both faithful and inclusive, and so on, often problems to which there seem to be no resolutions. This is where the practice of discernment becomes so important.

The Process of Discernment

The first step must always be to bring the problem to prayer, checking first one's own freedom to make sure that we are truly indifferent and open to what the Lord may want to show us. Then we need to lay the problem before the Lord with trust, asking the Lord's help. Discernment takes time; it can't be rushed. We need to live with a decision that seems to be emerging, to test it out, to see if imagining a movement in that direction brings peace.

St. Ignatius's teachings on discernment in the Exercises are helpful here; he says that the rules for discernment are different depending on where a person is in his or her own spiritual life. For those beginning the Exercises, making them for the first time, their primary call is usually to conversion of life.

That very challenge may call up fear, anxiety, and all sorts of imagined obstacles as well as filling the imagination with thoughts of enticing pleasures and sensual delights, signs of the evil spirit. In other words, the temptations are to what is obviously sinful and evil. However, the good spirit brings consolation, tears, quiet, and an easing of obstacles that gives one the courage to amend one's life (nos. 313–27).

The rules for the second and following weeks are different. For those making progress, moving into following Christ the King, the movements of the spirits are more subtle. Now the evil spirit—disguised as an angel of light—begins by suggesting thoughts more suited to someone growing in grace, holy and pious thoughts in conformity with the sanctity of the soul, and then little by little seeks to draw the person toward its own evil intentions. Here, the temptations are to things that are good—because obvious evil is not attractive to one growing in grace, but it is a lesser good, not the good intended by the Lord. So one clue is how the movement begins and where it ultimately seems to lead (no. 331).

Another clue is the way these movements are experienced affectively. The good spirit enters lightly and gently, like water being absorbed by a sponge, whereas the evil spirit enters with noise and disquiet, like water falling on a stone. For the person moving away from God, the signs are the reverse; the evil spirit is at home and so enters quietly, while the good spirit enters with noise and disruption because it is contrary to the disposition of the soul (no. 335).

Ignatius also talks about "consolation without cause," a movement of God that brings joy, peace, and a greater love of God without any particular experience or thought that might occasion such consolation. This is pure grace, God entering into soul where he is at home. Ignatius however also cautions that afterwards, while the consolation lingers, the person can be moved by either the good or evil spirit to resolutions not necessarily from God, and therefore is in need of discernment (nos. 330 and 336).

How do we discern which spirit is leading us when the discernment is among a variety of goods? Direction helps, simply having someone to talk to, to help process our experience, but also prayer, intimacy with God. Jesus' public ministry begins out of his own experience at the Jordan and his prayer and testing in the wilderness. If we too are to be led by the Spirit, to discern the spirit's presence, we must have a similar intimacy with God.

Reflection Questions

1. Where have I experienced the movement of the good spirit?

2. Do I habitually pray for interior freedom before attempting to make a difficult decision?

Notes: Day Six

1. Susan Bergman, *Martyrs: Contemporary Writers on Modern Lives of Faith* (Maryknoll, NY: Orbis Books, 1998).

2. Elaine Pagels, *The Gnostic Gospels* (New York: Random House, 1989), 146.

3. Cited in the *National Catholic Reporter,* 33 (September 12, 1997): 6.

4. See Kathleen Norris, *Cloister Walk* (New York: Riverhead Books, 1996), 116–23.

5. Wilkie Au and Noreen Cannon Au, *The Discerning Heart: Exploring the Christian Path* (Mahwah, NJ: Paulist Press, 2006), 139.

DAY 7

THE SEED MUST DIE

John 12:20–26

A number of years ago I drove across the country to Collegeville, Minnesota where I was spending the fall on sabbatical. I remember especially driving up through Utah and across the great plains of Wyoming and South Dakota enjoying the gorgeous vistas, great open sweeps of country, prairies and rolling hills under azure skies. The majestic country brought to my mind the great warrior culture of the Sioux, and I kept seeing them in my imagination, riding across the prairies I was passing through.

When I got to Collegeville, I found that even the stream that faced my apartment had once been the boundary separating the territories of the Sioux from those of the Osage. I began to read up on the Sioux. I reread the story of Pierre de Smedt, the great Jesuit missionary from Belgium so trusted by the Indians—even Sitting Bull was among his friends. I discovered the story of Black Elk, the Ogallala Sioux medicine man who was present at Little Big Horn and later traveled throughout Europe with Buffalo Bill's Wild West show, returning in time to be present—at a distance—at Wounded Knee. Black Elk told his story to a Nebraskan writer named John Neihardt who produced *Black Elk Speaks*, a classic if somewhat romanticized work about Native Americans.[1] But Neihardt neglects to tell his readers that Black Elk spent the last forty years of his life on the Pine Ridge Reservation as a catechist and was responsible for bringing hundreds of Native Americans into the Church. Perhaps it is more poetic and makes better drama to remember him as one of the last medicine men in a dying culture.

I read a great deal about the history of the Sioux: on the origins of their warrior culture and how the tribe had developed on the Great Plains. I learned about the games their children played, most of them geared to training boys to be warriors, to endure pain, to develop the warrior spirit. I read about Custer's great battle at Little Big Horn and about Wounded Knee where some two hundred Indians were tragically slaughtered in 1881, the results of mistakes that could have been avoided on both sides, supposedly after most of the "Indian Wars" had ended. And I read about their difficulty adjusting to a new way of life on the reservations: fed by the government, no longer independent, the warrior culture gone with the buffalo, the demoralization that set in and that still troubles many Native Americans in our country.

I was fascinated because the more I read, the more I experienced something of their loss, the sense that a whole world had been taken away and would never be again. It was like the death of a loved one. It took me a while to realize why that feeling was so strong and so familiar for me. Then I realized that I had often experienced similar feelings, about the Church, a Church which I have always loved.

A Changing Church

Our Church is in the process of changing. Many no longer practice their faith, and the Catholic culture that once supported them is gone. The institutional Church has lost much of its authority; many Catholics no longer give automatic assent to its teachings, or easily challenge its traditional positions. The priesthood too is changing. The old clerical culture is passing away. We can mourn its passing, but we can't preserve it. Tomorrow's Church will be much less hierarchical, less clerical, and more inclusive.

There was much about the old Church that I valued. It was too often an all-male world, a special place, privileged, and somewhat protected. Priests were special people, sacred ministers. Their clothing set them apart. So did the title, "Father." They were granted certain signs of respect. They were frequently asked for their blessings. There was camaraderie generated by long years of seminary living, cut off from the opposite sex, forced to define one's life exclusively in terms of the institution. It was the special world of the Church.

But there were many deficits to this clerical world. It was privileged and exclusive. It presumed special treatment. It encouraged careerism, the endless pursuit of a monsignor's biretta, a bishop's miter, a red hat. Some priests did not know how to relate to women, or to share their inner lives, their feelings and struggles with others, particularly with each other. We are familiar with the obvious signs of damage done to those who didn't cope well with this isolated world: the addictive behaviors, alcoholism, the naked pursuit of power, and the sexual abuse which has ruined so many lives, embarrassed the church, and scandalized the faithful. Other signs are less obvious. The loneliness that troubles many priests who are unable to develop real friendships with their fellow priests or with other men and women. I have seen this as a religious superior. I've heard priests in my community say as they grew older, "I don't have any close friends." "There is no one I can talk to."

There is no doubt that tomorrow's Church will be different, and it already asks different things of its priests: They must be able to work collaboratively with others, to share authority, and to listen to and accept criticism.

Those of us who are priests need to ask on what is our priestly identity based? To what extent are we dependent on a clerical culture for our support, on titles, dress, privilege, a certain splendid isolation? Or is our identity rooted somewhere deeper, in an awareness of discipleship, in constant prayer, in a supporting community?

Of course, these questions of identity and ministry are not just for priests. All those who experience a call to ministry in the Church face them in one way or another. Many religious men and women today face the diminishment of their communities. Some communities will disappear. But as Sean Sammon says, "Religious congregations were founded for mission not self-preservation; the real legacy of today's sisters, brothers, and priests is what their forbearers have always left behind: the next generation of believers, be they lay, ordained, or religious."[2]

Deacons and lay ministers can also seek to secure their identity in a particular office and function. They can be just as protective of their turf as any priest or bishop, just as legalistic in dealing with those who challenge their rules and procedures. They insist it's for the good of the Church, of course, or because it's liturgically correct, or because it's the way I want it. Clericalism is not something unique to Irish monsignors.

Living with Ambiguity

Can we as ministers live with the tension and ambiguity that always accompany a period of change? Can we allow others to make their own decisions? How do we handle disagreements?

I have a good friend with whom I was close when she was an undergraduate. After a year's service in a Christian volunteer program, she went on to medical school, taking gynecology as her specialty. We stayed in touch, and a few years ago I celebrated her marriage. A recent letter mentioning that she was working at an OBGYN outpatient clinic said something in passing about her finding that the "protestors" were really getting on her nerves; she admitted that they had a right to stand up for what they considered right, but was irritated by their harassment of patients and staff at her clinic.

I realized that she was working at a facility that included abortions among its procedures. I had previously some inkling that she might have some problems with the Church's position on abortion. Some years before she had said she didn't want to go to a Catholic medical school because she wanted to be instructed in all the procedures she should know as a physician, but this was the first clear indication that she might actually be involved in abortions herself.

What to do? I thought about it, prayed about it. Finally I wrote her a letter raising the issue. I asked her to help me to understand what she was doing. Her answer (later than usual; she was thinking about it), admitted that they did do some abortions at the clinic, that she had done some of these "procedures," and that she had conflicted feelings about it and about the Church's position, but felt that there were times when an abortion was necessary.

Why bring this up? Because we often experience such dilemmas as ministers. How do we respond? How should I have responded? Become judgmental? Condemn her for what she was doing? Drop her as a friend? There are many such people, good people close to us, who take positions very different than our own. We can cut off all those who don't agree with us, or we can try to find ways to witness to what we believe, to what we are committed to by the Church we serve, and pray that our witness and friendship might eventually help them come to a better decision. We can try to keep the conversation going or we can end the relationship. It is always better to build bridges than to break them down. We need to keep them in good repair. Ministers so judgmental in attitude that they cut off all who disagree with them or who won't let people come close, won't be able to be credible witnesses to the presence of Jesus and the kingdom. They certainly won't have many friends. We will not be good ministers if people can't get close enough to us to let us share their lives and struggles, even to tell us when they are doing things of which we can't approve. We can't really love at a distance. Love is messy; it means being willing to bear the pain of difference, disagreement, struggle, and the effort to be faithful.

Part of the painfulness of situations like this is that they make us vulnerable; when others make a different decision or do not hold to those values that we cherish, we tend to interpret it as a personal rejection or we feel less secure in our own position. That's why we want our friends to think like we do.

One important question we should ask ourselves is this: Are we able to live with a certain amount of ambiguity, give up our need to be in charge, to control others, events, the Church itself? Can we let others make their own decisions and continue to respect them, even when their decisions differ with our own, with what we believe to be right? Are we strong enough to hold to our Gospel values, even to be rejected for them, without becoming closed and bitter? Can we acknowledge our own weakness and vulnerability? Are we able to let go?

The Paschal Mystery

The paschal mystery is at the center of the Christian life. In the Synoptic Gospels Jesus repeatedly tells his disciples that they must be willing to take up the cross and come follow him; that the only way to save one's life is to lose it; that the last will be first and the first last. Paul speaks of the Christian as being baptized into the death of Jesus, so that just as he was raised from the dead, we too might live a new life (Rom 6:4). Challenging as these passages are, I've always preferred the passage from John where Jesus says simply, "unless a grain of wheat falls into the earth and dies, it remains just a single grain; but if it dies, it bears much fruit" (John 12:24). This sentence, phrased in the agricultural imagery of the countryside, sounds much more like Jesus. In it we hear his voice.

Reflection Questions

1. Where do I experience myself sharing in his paschal mystery?

2. What still needs to die in my life for the sake of my ministry?

THE PASSION OF JESUS

Isaiah 52:13–15; 53:1–12

It is not easy to contemplate the passion and death of Jesus.
There is something very stark, even painful about the story. Jesus
stands alone and defenseless before those who seek his life. The
fourth Servant Song of Second Isaiah captures something of the
feeling of Jesus in his passion:

> He was despised and rejected by others;
> a man of suffering and acquainted with infirmity;
> and as one from whom others hide their faces
> he was despised, and we held him of no account.
> Surely he has borne our infirmities
> and carried our diseases;
> yet we accounted him stricken,
> struck down by God, and afflicted.
> But he was wounded for our transgressions,
> crushed for our iniquities;
> upon him was the punishment that made us whole,
> and by his bruises we are healed.
> All we like sheep have gone astray;
> we have all turned to our own way,
> and the Lord has laid on him
> the iniquity of us all. (Isa 53:3–6)

In the final days of his ministry Jesus must have experienced a growing sense of failure. The increasing hostility of the

religious authorities, particularly the Temple priesthood was obvious. He was well aware of what had happened to his mentor, John the Baptist. Matthew tells us that when Jesus heard of John's death, he withdrew into a deserted place by himself (Matt 13:13). The predictions of the passion in the Gospels were shaped by the early communities in light of his death, but Jesus certainly would have seen it coming.

A Final Confrontation

His entry into Jerusalem is followed in the Synoptic accounts by the story of the cleansing of the Temple, overturning the tables of the money changers and the stalls of those selling animals (Mark 11:15–19). The story is often seen as an act of out-raged piety against those who had turned the house of God into a den of thieves, perhaps an echo of Jeremiah 7:11. But many scholars today believe his action had a much deeper meaning, that it was a prophetic act against the Temple itself and its cult that could not function without the animals used for sacrifice. It reflects a final confrontation with the religious leaders.

In doing this, Jesus was striking against the central religious institution of Judaism, closing down at least temporarily its cult, provocatively symbolizing that its time was at an end, that it would be destroyed, just as at his trial before the Sanhedrin he was charged with saying he would destroy the Temple (Mark 14:58). Mark's story of Jesus cursing the fig tree for its lack of fruit (Mark 11:20–25), the only destructive miracle of Jesus, symbolizes God's judgment on the Temple, with its lack of fruit (cf. Jer 8:13). The true Israel is not the Israel centered on the Temple and ruled by the priests, but the eschatological community of salvation, the new family of those who hear the word of God and do it (Mark 3:35; Luke 8:21). This of course was a direct challenge to the authority of Israel's religious leaders; they had to get rid of him.

The Last Supper

Knowing that his time was at hand, Jesus gathered the Twelve for a final meal, the Passover supper according to the Synoptic tradition. The disciples had shared many meals together; this one would have been more solemn. Luke captures something of its pathos, quoting Jesus as saying "I have eagerly desired to eat this Passover with you before I suffer" (Luke 22:15). In the course of it, Jesus took the bread, broke it, and said "This is my body, which is given for you. Do this in remembrance of me." In the same way he took the cup, saying "This cup that is poured out for you is the new covenant in my blood" (Luke 22: 19–20). While his words have been shaped by the liturgy of the Church, the association of the bread and cup of wine with his body broken and blood to be poured out can have come only from Jesus.

But then he said something that did not become part of the liturgy and is recognized by many scholars as authentic. He told the Twelve, "I will never again drink of the fruit of the vine until that day when I drink it new in the kingdom of God" (Mark 14:25). In other words, in the face of his death, he promises his disciples a renewed fellowship with himself beyond it. However hidden the future was for Jesus, he does not see his death as the end. He remained confident that God's reign would come about in spite of it, or even more, through it. The later Church was to see his accepting his death in faithfulness to his mission of proclaiming God's reign as a sacrifice, for his death thus becomes part of his mission. He did not go to his death unaware of its meaning.

The story of the two disciples on the road to Emmaus suggests that the disciples continued Jesus' practice of table fellowship after his death, mindful of the Last Supper tradition, and so came to recognize him present among them in a new way; "he had been made known to them in the breaking of the bread"

(Luke 24:35). This is how Christians have come to recognize him down through the centuries.

The Eucharist holds pride of place in the Church's life as it offers a unique encounter with the risen Jesus. Think for a moment of the two most intimate forms of union for human beings. One is sexual intercourse in which the union of two spirits is symbolized in the physical union of their bodies, each giving themselves to the other without reservation. In the words of scripture, the two become one flesh (Gen 2:24). It is a union of love that is literally life giving.

The other is the act of eating in which we take into ourselves that which is external to us, the fruits of the earth and the work of human hands which literally becomes part of us. We are what we eat! In the Eucharist, in our partaking of the bread broken and the cup poured out, we become ourselves the body of Christ. It too is a union of love, an intimate union of the risen Jesus with his own. Jesus gives himself mystically as he gave himself historically, completely. Our communion in his body and blood gives us new life as his Body for the world (cf. 1 Cor 10:16–17).

The Crucifixion

When we have grown up with the crucifix as a familiar symbol of the faith it's difficult to grasp its horror as an instrument of torture and death. The humiliation of the cross, the body spread naked for all to see, was used by the Romans as a brutal form of capital punishment reserved for slaves, criminals, and those who rebelled against imperial authority.

Too many emphasize the divinity of Jesus at the expense of his humanity; they attribute divine knowledge to him and assume that he was fully aware of his ultimate victory. Thus they miss the full cost of his passion.

St. Ignatius invites the retreatant contemplating the passion to consider how "the divinity hides itself" (no. 196), leaving Jesus vulnerable in his humanity. His body wracked by pain, made a public spectacle, mocked by the crowd, and deserted by his friends, his cry from the cross, "My God, my God, why have you forsaken me?" (Mark 15:34) suggests that he felt abandoned even by his God. Having entered into our humanity, he entered into it fully, even into that the dark night of the spirit that all of us experience at times. Accepting even death was God's yes to our humanity in all its frailty (cf. 2 Cor 1:18–19). As Dean Brackley says, "Precisely by hiding itself...the divinity reveals its greater splendor. It reveals God's complete solidarity with our weakness and suffering."[3]

I've often noticed how those who are close to death, even those of very deep faith, seem to experience an absence of God; often they are unable to pray on their own and welcome those who will help them pray. God seems absent; he seems to withdraw, leaving them without resources. Jesus in his agony must have experienced this utter abandonment. As Walter Kasper says, "Jesus experienced the unfathomable mystery of God and his will, but he endured this darkness in faith. This extremity of emptiness enabled him to become the vessel of God's fullness."[4]

Thus we can say that Jesus faced his own death with all the fear and uncertainty that any human facing death experiences, and yet he did not despair. He continued to trust, to cling in faith to the one he called "Abba," even though the Father did not intervene in his desperate moment. He died as he had lived, not letting go of the Abba who would not let go of him, and so he shows us that God's love is stronger than death.

Suggestions for Prayer

Sit quietly with some aspect of the passion, reading one of the accounts slowly, or take some time to contemplate the cross. Realize that the passion of Jesus is still taking place today.

Notes: Day Seven

1. John G. Neihardt, *Black Elk Speaks* (Lincoln, NE: University of Nebraska Press, 1970).

2. Sean D. Sammon, *An Undivided Heart: Making Sense of Celibate Chastity* (New York: Alba House, 1993), 20.

3. Dean Brackley, *The Call to Discernment in Troubled Times* (New York: Crossroad, 2004), 182.

4. Walter Kasper, *Jesus the Christ* (New York: Paulist Press, 1976), 118–19.

DAY 8

THE RESURRECTION

John 21:15–18

How do we enter into the joy of the resurrection? In the fourth week of the *Spiritual Exercises,* St. Ignatius asks the retreatant to consider how the divinity of Jesus, so hidden during the passion, now manifests itself in his resurrection. And he presents the retreatant with a contemplation of Christ appearing first to his mother, referring to her simply as Our Lady. Though this mystery is not in scripture, Ignatius's impulse here is certainly not foreign to the Christian tradition.

Christ's Easter appearance to Mary can be found in the Eastern Church as early as the fourth century in St. Ephrem's commentary on Taitian's *Diatesseron,* preserved in classical Armenian. Though Ephrem has confused Mary the Mother of Jesus with Mary Magdalene due to an error in the biblical manuscript he was using, he takes an appearance of the risen Jesus to his mother for granted, rightly considering her as receiving the "first-fruits" of her son's return from the dead. This tradition entered the Byzantine liturgy in the fifth century through the influence of St. Romanus Melodus. Ignatius encountered the tradition in Ludolph the Carthusian's *Life of Christ.* But he may have been aware of it from other sources. He may well have been familiar with fifteenth- and sixteenth-century guidebooks for pilgrims to Jerusalem, all of which recommended a visit to "the chapel of the Blessed Virgin Mary" where this appearance was supposed to have taken place.[1]

In introducing this contemplation, Ignatius speaks of Christ, the risen Lord exercising the role of consoler, just as friends are accustomed to console one another. He encourages the retreatant in this final week to pray for the grace of intense joy and gladness with Christ, the risen Lord (no. 221). His words appeal to us. We want to share the Easter joy and exaltation of the disciples, we want to know the risen Jesus. But praying over the mystery of the resurrection is often difficult. If we can understand the Easter experience of the disciples, it is not so easy to experience the joy ourselves.

The Easter Stories

Edward Schillebeeckx stresses that the disciples had a real experience of Jesus as the risen one, but he stresses, as do most theologians, that the Easter stories in the Gospels are far more theological lessons than historical accounts. A careful reading of the gospel appearance stories suggests the same; the disciples react to the risen Jesus with hesitation and fear; they don't recognize him; they think that they are seeing a ghost. Some continue to doubt (Matt 28:17). One senses that Jesus has to lead them to recognition and belief (cf. Luke 24:38–43). Not even Mary Magdalene, who was so close to him, recognizes him at first; she thinks he is the gardener (John 20:15).

Still the Easter stories have much to teach us. They are written specifically to help those in the early Christian churches encounter the risen Jesus and come to faith in him. Thus, they teach that Jesus is to be encountered in the community of the

Church (Matt 28:20), the breaking of the bread (Luke 24:35), and the forgiveness of sins (John 20:23). John's Gospel stresses that one does not have to see in order to believe (John 20:29).

An Experience of Forgiveness

John's story of Peter's encounter with the risen Jesus on the shores of the Sea of Galilee suggests something profound about Peter's own religious experience (John 21:15–18). How did he encounter the risen Lord? Peter, always in charge, so often boastful and self-confident, at the same time was terribly lacking in self-knowledge. At the Last Supper he proclaimed that he was ready to die with Jesus. But in the courtyard of the high priest when a servant girl asked if he was one of Jesus' band, three times he denied that he even knew him. How broken-hearted Peter must have been for he truly loved Jesus; he knew he had failed him. Luke tells us that after Peter's betrayal Jesus turned and looked at him, and Peter went out and began to weep bitterly (Luke 22:61–62).

Peter, like Judas, must have been tempted to despair. But he didn't, and according to at least one tradition, he was the first to whom the risen Jesus appeared. John's story of the miraculous catch of fish and breakfast by the Sea of Galilee deliberately recalls the scene of his betrayal. In John's account Peter denies Jesus three times before a charcoal fire. At the lake shore, again there is a charcoal fire, and three times Peter must repeat, "Lord, you know that I love you." So the appearance scene mimics that of the betrayal, but here Peter is forgiven, rehabilitated, restored to his place, and made shepherd of the flock.

Whatever the historicity of this particular story, all the Gospels tell of Peter's betrayal. Certainly the experience of being forgiven for the offense for which he could not forgive himself must have been basic to his own encounter with the risen Jesus.

Peter's sense of meeting the risen Jesus was inseparable from a profound experience of forgiveness and reconciliation. In the eyes of Jesus his sin does not count; only the Lord's love for him is real, and that love changed his life and enabled the blundering Peter of the Gospels to become one of the great apostles of the primitive church.

An Experience of Liberation

We have an even clearer sense of who Paul was, both before and after his meeting with the risen Lord because Paul is the only New Testament author who writes autobiographically. Saul of Tarsus, as he was originally known, was something of a religious fanatic, a man of strong character and passionate single-mindedness, trained as a Pharisee in the law, so obsessed with his own understanding of his tradition, his own theology, that he became a persecutor of some of his fellow Jews who were disciples of Jesus. He could not abide their confessing him as messiah and Lord, risen from the dead. According to the Acts of the Apostles, Saul was implicated in the stoning of Stephen (Acts 7:58) and afterwards began a persecution of the disciples that was to be long remembered (Acts 9:1–2). His extreme reaction to the early disciples suggests that he shared some of the narrowness and inflexibility of the compulsive religious personality.

It would be a mistake to attribute this compulsive character and fanaticism to his background as a Pharisee. Not all the Pharisees were fanatics. Among them were wise men like Gamaliel who advised the Sanhedrin not to use violence against the disciples, arguing that if their movement was not from God it would not long endure (Acts 5:38). The Pharisees' emphasis on the law may have reinforced the legalism that was a part of Paul's own personality, but it did not cause it. His rigidity was the shadow side of his strong character; it was rooted in his own personal makeup and in his personal religious needs.

Yet in spite of his intolerance, Paul was a deeply religious man. The great issue of his life, both as a Pharisee and later as a Christian was righteousness before God. He thought he had discovered the way to that righteousness in the teaching of the Pharisees, and prided himself on his being "as to righteous under the law, blameless" (Phil 3:6). But his life was radically changed by his experience of meeting the risen Jesus. This man, Paul the legalist and defender of the law, became the apostle of justification by faith rather than by works of the law (Rom 3:28; Gal 2:16). One senses something of the personal liberation Paul experienced, of being set free from his own rigidity and perfectionism, in the emphasis on freedom that became so much a part of his preaching. He uses that lovely expression, "the glorious freedom of the children of God" (Rom 8:21 NAB), and taught that in Christ Christians enjoyed a threefold freedom, freedom from the obligations of the law (Rom 7:3 ff.), freedom from sin (Rom 6:18–23), and as a consequence, freedom from death itself (Rom 6:21).

Paul experienced this freedom first of all in his own life, freed as he was through grace of his compulsive need to justify himself, to win God's approval through his legal observance. The change that came over him was not easy, as it meant giving up a tradition to which he was passionately attached. But his experience of meeting the risen Jesus left him a different man, gentled in spirit, ready to accept and even to boast of his own weakness, for it was only in owning his weakness that he became aware of the power of Christ working through him (2 Cor 12:9–10).

A Personal Experience

We often speak of meeting the risen Jesus in others—in the poor, the suffering—and sometimes we have a sense of his presence. But personally I have often found that language difficult. Our hopes so often outdistance what we actually experience. We get caught up in the mundane; the eyes of our spirits are often dim. Yet I recently had an experience that, on reflection, struck me as a genuine experience of the Jesus who lives and continues to care for us.

It was during a retreat. I had taken the quiet afternoon hours for a hike up a mountain trail that took off from behind the retreat house. It was quite steep, and though I consider myself to be in pretty good condition, I was puffing on the way up, and when I finally got to the top and paused, it was not just to admire the splendid view. I was winded, out of breath. After resting for a bit, I began back down the trail. About half way down, I passed a young family of four on the way up, a mother, father, and two young children. The father was carrying his younger son on his shoulders.

We exchanged a greeting, and as I continued down, I was suddenly struck with a wonderful appreciation of what this young man was doing, taxing his own energy with the additional weight of his tired little boy. And I suddenly had a sense that this was a perfect image of Jesus' love for us—Jesus who so often carries us, who has added our burdens to his own, who has taken our sins upon himself, who is completely for us. I had the clear sense that I had encountered the Lord in meeting howsoever briefly that family on the mountain trail. Perhaps this is another kind of Easter experience.

A Final Word

In speaking of the contemplation of Christ's appearance to his mother with which we began, Father Jean Laplace points to her participation in the paschal mystery as being at the heart of this experience. What he says is true of all who share in that mystery: "They have become one in heart: at the foot of the cross, Mary united herself to the intention of her Son. It is this presence in the Spirit that constitutes their unity. It is this presence that the Resurrection has brought about: Christ is present to those who are united with him in their heart."[2]

Reflection Questions

1. Where have I encountered the risen Lord?

2. Where have I been surprised by joy, or love, or faithfulness?

3. Where have I experienced new life and hope?

4. Where has my life been changed and transformed by the experience of meeting Jesus?

CONTEMPLATIO AD AMOREM

Psalm 138

At the end of the *Spiritual Exercises,* Ignatius proposes a meditation called the *Contemplatio ad amorem,* the Contemplation for Obtaining Love (nos. 230–37). It invites us into the imaginative contemplation that is so typical of Ignatius, a contemplation that seeks to make contact with God through our human experience, our affectivity, and our imaginations. In many ways it serves as a resumé of the *Exercises* themselves, and so can serve as a way of bringing our retreat to a close.

Before beginning the exercise, Ignatius asks the retreatant to consider two points: first, that love ought to manifest itself in deeds rather than in words. And second, that love consists in a mutual sharing of gifts (nos. 230–31). The *Contemplatio* itself is built around four points.

First, Ignatius invites us to consider all the favors we have received from God: in creation, in redemption, and in our concrete gifts. I might take this as an occasion to reflect on my own life, reviewing its different stages, seeing how God has been a part of it since my earliest days or at particular moments. I might think of how my parents gave me life and formed me through their love and presence; the gifts God has given me in my siblings, grandparents, and other members of my family; the friendships that have nurtured me and helped me to grow over the years. I might think of my own faith journey, of moments when

I've felt God's nearness in a special way, or in which I've been particularly blessed. I might think of the gifts of mind, body, and personality that are mine, all those things that bring me joy and a sense of well-being.

Second, we are to consider how God dwells in his creatures, giving them life, sensation, understanding, and in our own case, making us in the image and likeness of the divine majesty. Let me consider for a moment the splendor of the created world: the night sky bright with an incredible number of stars; the wonderful diversity of the animal kingdom; the beauty of the human face and body that reflects the beauty of the creator; the power of the music of a Beethoven or the breathtaking art of a Michelangelo, a Titian, or a van Gogh. Let me recall how God has been present in the love I have experienced from dear friends, or how the light of my own intelligence is a participation in the uncreated light of God.

Third, Ignatius invites us to consider how God toils and labors in all created things, conducting "Himself after the manner of one who labors." Let me imagine the incredible power of nature, the tiny slip of a pine tree forcing its way through the rock of a hillside or the restless energy of the ocean. Consider, for example, how nature is constantly seeking ways to preserve life, to reproduce, to flourish. I might consider Teilhard de Chardin's vision of how matter itself has evolved over its long history, developing ever more complex forms, atomic and chemical structures, molecules and cellular life, then ever more complex living forms that can support greater degrees of consciousness, and ultimately self-consciousness in the emergence of the human, all reflecting God's creative power, working from within created reality.

Consider God's work of creation in Genesis 1, God who delights in his work, repeatedly calling it good, and resting from his labor on the seventh day (Gen 2:4), and realize that God is sustaining all creation and my own existence in this very instant. Or read contemplatively Psalm 104, which praises God's work in caring for his creation, spreading the heavens like a tent-cloth, watering the mountains, giving drink to all the beasts, raising grass for the cattle, producing bread from the earth and wine to warm men's hearts. Even Leviathan, the mythological monster of the pagan creation narrative, now plays in the sea that God formed.

The final point is to consider how all good gifts come from above, reflecting in some way the goodness, power, mercy, and justice of God. I might consider the innocence in the face of a child, the goodness of people who have touched me in special ways, the times I have been moved by acts of self-sacrifice or graciousness or compassion, the tender care of a mother for her child, the love in the eyes of a dear friend. Our memories are rich storehouses of sights, sounds, feelings, and emotions that speak to us of the goodness, presence, and love of God. Our senses open us to the beauty of the world, our minds marvel at the immensity of creation, and our spirits reach out to embrace the God who has so blessed us, and so we can indeed find God in all things.

To each point, we are invited to respond, using the prayer that has become known as the "Suscipe":

Take, Lord, and receive all my liberty, my memory, my understanding, and my entire will—all I have and possess. You have given all to me, and I return it, Lord, to you. Everything is yours; dispose of it only according to your will. Give me your love and your grace; for me, that is enough.

Reflection Questions

1. What are some of the gifts of God for which I am most grateful?

2. How has God shown me his special love?

3. What return can I make to the Lord for all that he has given to me?

Notes: Day Eight

1. Carl F. Starkloff, ed., *The Road from La Storta: Peter-Hans Kolvenbach, S.J., on Ignatian Spirituality* (St. Louis: Institute of Jesuit Sources, 2000), 49ff.

2. Jean Laplace, *An Experience of Life in the Spirit: Ten Days in the Tradition of the Spiritual Exercises* (Chicago: Franciscan Herald Press, 1977), 172.

SCRIPTURE TEXTS

DAYS 1–2

Exod 3:4–7 — holy ground

Pss 16, 17, 23, 25, 27, 31, 42–43, 103, 104, 119, 138, 139 — psalms

1 Sam 3:1–18 — speak, Lord, your servant is listening

Job 38 — Yahweh's answer from the whirlwind

Isa 40:1–11 — comfort my people

Isa 43:1–8 — you are precious

Isa 45:7–13 — God's creative work; let justice descend

Isa 49:8–18 — mother and child; upon the palm

Isa 55:1–6 — all who are thirsty; seek the Lord

Isa 61:1–11 — Spirit of the Lord

Jer 1:4–10 — Jeremiah's call

Mic 6:6–8 — three things I ask

Wis 9:1–18 — give me wisdom, the attendant at your throne

Ezek 36:16–30 — new heart and new spirit

Rom 8:14–17, 26–27 — Spirit searches our hearts

2 Cor 4:1–11 — apostolic ministry; light on face of Christ

Ps 51 — turn away your face from my sins

DAY 3

Incarnation — text from *Spiritual Exercises*

Ezek 16	Jerusalem as abandoned child
Isa 11:1–9	Christmas introit
John 1:1–14	prologue
Matt 1:18–25	Joseph's dilemma
Luke 2:1–14	nativity
Phil 2:6–11	*kenosis*
Luke 2:22–38	presentation
Luke 2:51–52	hidden life
Wis 2:12–24	just man

DAY 4

Luke 3:21–22	baptism of Jesus
John 1:29–34	baptism and Spirit
John 1:35–42	call of Andrew and Simon
John 1:43–51	call of Nathaniel
Luke 4:1–13	temptations
Luke 5:1–11	miraculous catch; call of Peter
Mark 1:29–39	Simon's mother-in-law; dawn prayer
Mark 3:1–6	man with withered hand
Mark 10:17–27	rich man
Luke 6:17–26	Beatitudes
Matt 5:1–11	Beatitudes
Luke 6:27–47	continuation of sermon on plain
Matt 12:22–32	Jesus and Beelzebul; sin against Holy Spirit

DAYS 5–6

John 2:1–12	Cana
John 3:1–17	Nicodemus
John 4:4–42	Samaritan woman
John 10:1–16	good shepherd
John 11:1–44	raising of Lazarus
John 12:12–19	entry into Jerusalem

John 12:20–36	seed must die
Mark 2:13–17	Levi; table fellowship
Mark 4:35–41	storm at sea
Mark 5:1–20	Gerasene demoniac
Mark 6:34–44	miracle of the loaves
Mark 8:27–33	Peter's confession
Mark 8:34–38	conditions for discipleship
Mark 8:27—10:52	way section
Mark 9:2–8	transfiguration
Mark 14:3–9	anointing at Bethany
Matt 13	parables of the kingdom
Matt 20:1–16	workers in the field
Luke 7:36–50	woman who weeps
Luke 8:1–8	parable of the seed
Luke 9:1–6	twelve and the reign of God
Luke 19:1–7	Zacchaeus
Luke 10:29–37	good Samaritan
Luke 11:1–13	Lord's prayer; persistence in prayer
Luke 15:11–32	prodigal son
Luke 20:28–40	entry into Jerusalem
2 Cor 3–5	apostolic ministry

DAY 7

Mark 14:27–31	prediction of Peter's betrayal
Luke 20:41–44	Jesus weeps over Jerusalem
Luke 22:7–20	Last Supper
John 13:1–17	washing of feet
Mark 14:32–52	agony in the garden
Isa 52:13–53	suffering servant

DAY 8

Gen 1:1—2:4a	gifts of creation
Pss 104, 138	nature